STEM Labs for Physical Science
Grades 6–8

Authors: Schyrlet Cameron and Carolyn Craig
Editor: Mary Dieterich
Proofreaders: April Albert and Margaret Brown

COPYRIGHT © 2017 Mark Twain Media, Inc.

ISBN 978-1-62223-641-1

Printing No. CD-404262

Mark Twain Media, Inc., Publishers
Distributed by Carson-Dellosa Publishing LLC

MAR 2 9 2018

Visit us at www.carsondellosa.com

Table of Contents

To the Teacher

STEM is an acronym for **Science, Technology, Engineering,** and **Mathematics**. STEM education is an initiative designed to get students interested in these career fields. STEM learning emphasizes students gaining knowledge and developing skills needed for a twenty-first-century workforce.

STEM Labs is a three-book series. The books in the series include *STEM Labs for Life Science, STEM Labs for Physical Science,* and *STEM Labs for Earth & Space Science.* The series provides fun and meaningful integrated activities designed to cultivate student interest in topics of the STEM fields. All the activities in the series are lab investigations that support the national standards: Next Generation Science Standards (NGSS) developed by the National Teachers of Science Association (NTSA), National Council of Teachers of Mathematics Standards (NCTM), Standards for Technology Literacy (ITEA), and Common Core State Standards (CCSS). Each book includes:

- **Instructional Resources:** A set of informational handouts to guide students in successfully completing STEM investigations.
- **Lab Challenges:** Investigations promoting the STEM fields (science, technology, engineering, and mathematics). Labs emphasize designing an object, process, model, or system to solve a problem.
- **Rubrics:** Scoring guides explain the set of criteria used for assessing the projects.

STEM Labs for Physical Science contains 26 lab activities that challenge students to apply scientific inquiry, content knowledge, and technological design to solve a real-world problem. Key components of every lab activity are creativity, teamwork, communication, and critical-thinking. Each lab activity requires students to:

- **Research:** Students find out what is already known about the topic being investigated.
- **Collaborate:** Students complete activities in collaborative groups. They are encouraged to communicate openly, support each other, and respect contributions of members as they pool perspectives and experiences toward solving a problem.
- **Design:** Students use creativity and imagination to design an object, process, model, or system. Students test the design, record data, and analyze and interpret results.
- **Reflect:** Students think back on the process in a way that further promotes higher-order thinking.

STEM Labs for Physical Science is written for classroom teachers, parents, and students. This book can be used to supplement existing curriculum or enhance after-school or summer-school programs.

STEM Education

The STEMs of Learning: **Science**, **Technology**, **Engineering**, and **Mathematics** is an initiative designed to get students interested in these career fields. In 2009, the National Academy of Engineering (NAE) and the National Research Council (NRC) reported that there was a lack of focus on the science, technology, engineering, and mathematics (STEM) subjects in K–12 schools. This creates concerns about the competitiveness of the United States in the global market and the development of a workforce with the knowledge and skills needed to address technical and technological issues.

STEM Education	
STEM	**Knowledge and Skills Needed to Address Technical and Technological Issues**
Science	**Basic science process skills** include the basic skills of classifying, observing, measuring, inferring, communicating, predicting, manipulating materials, replicating, using numbers, developing vocabulary, questioning, and using cues. **Integrated science skills** (more complex skills) include creating models, formulating a hypothesis, generalizing, identifying and controlling variables, defining operationally, recording and interpreting data, making decisions, and experimenting.
Technology	**Design process** includes identifying and collecting information about everyday problems that can be solved by technology. It also includes generating ideas and requirements for solving the problems.
Engineering	**Design process** includes identifying a problem or design opportunity; proposing designs and possible solutions; implementing the solution; evaluating the solution and its consequences; and communicating the problem, processes, and solution.
Mathematics	**Mathematical skills** include the ability to use problem-solving skills, formulate problems, develop and apply a variety of strategies to solve problems, verify and interpret results, and generalize solutions and strategies to new problems. Students also need to be able to communicate with models, orally, in writing, and with pictures and graphs; reflect and clarify their own thinking; use the skills of reading, listening, and observing to interpret and evaluate ideas; and be able to make conjectures and convincing arguments.

Characteristics of a STEM Lesson

STEM education emphasizes a new way of teaching and learning that focuses on hands-on inquiry and open-ended exploration. It allows students with diverse interests, abilities, and experiences to develop skills they will need in the 21st-century workforce. It is a shift away from the teacher presenting information and covering science topics to the teacher guiding and assisting students in problem-solving while encouraging them to take the lead in their own learning.

Characteristics of a STEM Lesson

- Stimulates the curiosity and interest of both girls and boys
- Emphasizes hands-on, inquiry-based learning
- Addresses both math and science standards
- Encourages the use of and/or creation of technology
- Involves the engineering design process
- Stresses collaborative teamwork

---

10 Steps in a STEM Lesson

Students are presented with a challenge to design a model, process, or system to solve a problem. They work on the challenge in collaborative teams of three or four students, depending on the STEM lesson. Each team follows a set of problem-solving steps in order to find a solution.

Step #1:   Research the problem and solutions.

Step #2:   Brainstorm ideas about how to design a model, process, or system to solve the problem.

Step #3:   Draw a diagram of the model, process, or system.

Step #4:   Construct a prototype.

Step #5:   Test the prototype.

Step #6:   Evaluate the performance of the prototype.

Step #7:   Identify how to improve the design of the prototype.

Step #8:   Make the needed changes to the prototype.

Step #9:   Retest and reevaluate the prototype.

Step #10:   Share the results.

Introduction to STEM

Collaborative Learning Teams

Collaborative learning is a successful teaching strategy in which small groups of students, each with different levels of ability and diverse interests and experiences, work together to solve a problem, complete a task, or create a product. The responsibility for learning is placed squarely on the shoulders of the students. Each student is individually accountable for their own work, and the work of the group as a whole is also evaluated. The role of the teacher is to guide and assist the students in the problem-solving process. A collaborative learning environment in the science classroom has many benefits.

Benefits of Collaborative Learning
- Engages students in active learning
- Encourages students to communicate openly
- Motivates students to cooperate and support each other
- Teaches respect for contributions of all members
- Prepares students for the real world

Team Dynamics

It is important that the teacher organizes the classroom into teams. Teams should consist of three or four students, depending on the STEM activity. Fewer members may limit the diversity of ideas, skills, and approaches to problem-solving.

Assigning Roles

A successful collaborative learning experience requires a division of the workload among the members of a team. The teacher may wish to assign the role of each member of the team as follows:

- **Team Captain** is responsible for keeping the group on-task.

- **Recorder** is responsible for organizing the paperwork and creating drawings, diagrams, or illustrations as needed.

- **Materials Manager** is responsible for gathering the needed materials and supplies for the project.

- **Monitor** is responsible for keeping the work area tidy and for properly storing the project at the end of the class.

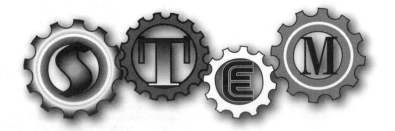

STEM: Preparing Students for the 21st Century

Recent shifts in education are being driven by colleges and businesses demanding that high school graduates have the "21st-century skills" necessary for success in today's world. They are advocating schools teach students certain core competencies such as collaboration, critical thinking, and problem-solving. STEM education focuses on these skills and, at the same time, fosters student interests in the fields of science, technology, engineering, and mathematics.

Why STEM Education?

STEM Promotes:
- student-centered learning.
- collaboration and teamwork.
- equality (equally benefits boys and girls).
- critical-thinking skills.
- hands-on, inquiry-based learning.
- use of technology.
- engineering design process.
- opportunities to apply math skills and knowledge.
- greater depth of subject exploration.
- innovation.
- real-world problem solving.
- curiosity and creativity.
- teachers as facilitators and monitors of learning.

Common Hurdles to STEM Education

STEM Requires:
- students have baseline skills in reading, math, and science to be successful.
- students be able to work well with others.
- flexible lesson plans; projects may take one class period to several weeks to complete.

The Pieces of STEM

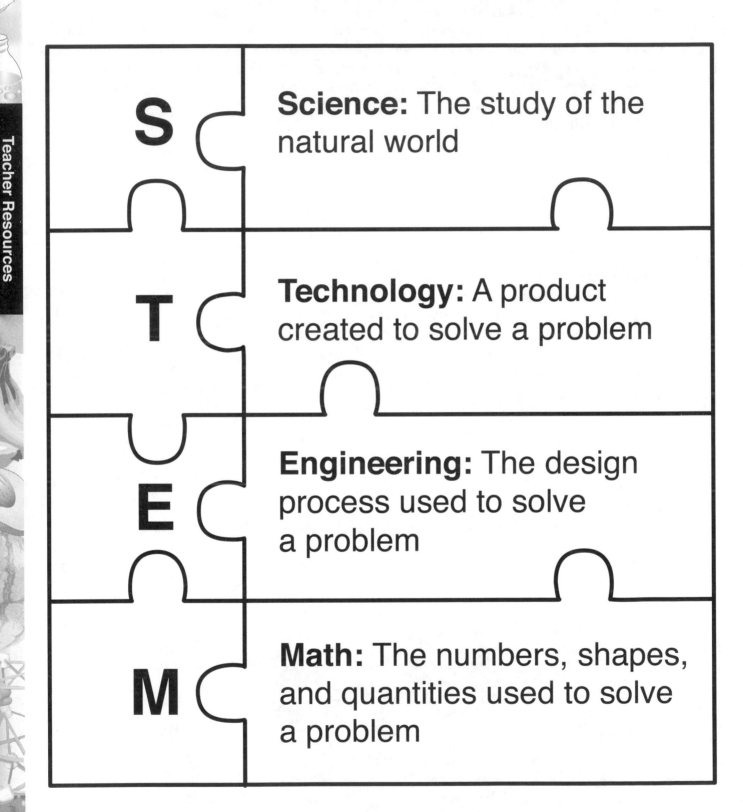

Science: The study of the natural world

Technology: A product created to solve a problem

Engineering: The design process used to solve a problem

Math: The numbers, shapes, and quantities used to solve a problem

10 Tips for Student Collaboration

1. Respect Each Other and All Ideas

2. No "Put Downs"

3. Be a Good, Active Listener

4. Come Well Prepared for Task Assignment

5. Participate and Contribute During Discussions

6. Support Your Opinions

7. Promote Positive Team-Member Relations

8. Disagree in an Agreeable Manner

9. Encourage Team Members

10. Complete Tasks on Time and With Quality Work

Name: _____   Date: _____

STEM Lab Challenge Rubric

Task	4	3	2	1
Research	Demonstrates planned technological and other research/inquiry that leads to educated decisions; All information cited following copyright guidelines	Demonstrates technological and other research/inquiry; Most information cited	Demonstrates some technological and other research/inquiry; Some information cited	Demonstrates no technological and other research/inquiry; No information cited
Model Process or System	Drawing has labels and advanced explanation of strategy	Drawing has labels and explanation of strategy	Drawing has some labels and partial explanation of strategy	Drawing has no labels or explanation of strategy
Results	All records, analysis, and interpretation of test results in organized, accurate manner	Records, analysis, and interpretation of test results completed	Records, analysis, and/ or interpretation of test results incomplete	No records, analysis, or interpretation of test results
Conclusion	Demonstrates high-level thinking when summarizing the purpose, test procedure, and test results	Demonstrates thinking skills summarizing the purpose, test procedure, and test results	Demonstrates some thinking skills summarizing the purpose, test procedure, and test results	Demonstrates no thinking skills summarizing the purpose, test procedure, and test results
Reflection	Reflection completed with thoughtful insight into team's choices	Reflection completed with insignt into team's choices	Reflection partially completed with little insight into team's choices	Reflection incomplete
Evaluation	Self-evaluation completed with thoughtful insights about behavior and performance as a team member	Self-evaluation completed with insights	Self-evaluation partially completed; some insights	Self-evaluation incomplete—no insights

Teacher Comments:

Name: _____   **STEM Lab Self-Evaluation Rubric**   Date: _____

Directions: Circle the description in each category that you believe best describes your behavior and performance during the assigned lab challenge.

Category	4	3	2	1
Attitude	Always positive attitude about the challenge; never critical of the project or the work of other team members	Mostly positive attitude about the challenge; rarely critical of the project or the work of other team members	Usually positive attitude about the challenge; sometimes critical of the project or the work of other team members	Negative attitude about the challenge; often critical of the project or the work of other team members
Work Quality	Highest quality work	High quality work	Work occasionally needs to be redone by others to ensure quality	Work needs to be redone by others to ensure quality
Innovative Problem-solving	Seeks multiple, innovative solutions to the problem to meet the challenge	Seeks some innovative solutions to the problem to meet the challenge	Seeks a few possible solutions to the problem to meet the challenge	Seeks no solutions to the problem to meet the challenge
Contributions	Consistently works to fulfill challenge requirements and perform individual team-member role	Frequently works to fulfill challenge requirements and perform individual team-member role	Sometimes works to fulfill challenge requirements and perform individual team-member role	Seldom works to fulfill challenge requirements and perform individual team-member role
Lab Focus	Focuses with team members to complete the lab challenge without having to be reminded; self-directed	Focuses with team members to complete the lab challenge; rarely needs reminding; reliable team member	Sometimes focuses with team members to complete the lab challenge; often needs reminding; unreliable team member	Seldom focuses with team members to completer the lab challenge; often disruptive; unreliable team member

Student Comments:

Teacher Resources

Reflection

Name: _____ Date: _____

Title of Lab Challenge: _____

Directions: Complete the following statements about your lab challenge.

One thing I didn't expect from this challenge was	If I want to get better at scientific investigation, I need to
One thing I would improve if I did this lab again would be	One thing I would like to learn more about after doing this investigation is
After completing this challenge, I realize that	The hardest part of this investigation was

From completing this investigative lab, I now understand

Enteric-Coated Pills: Teacher Information

STEM Lab Overview
Students are challenged to design an enteric-coated pill. The pill must withstand the acidic environment of the human stomach for 10 minutes.

Concepts	
• Acid and bases	• Human digestive system

Standards for Grades 6–8			
NGSS	**NCTM**	**ITEA**	**CCSS**
-Structure and Properties of Matter	-Problem Solving -Communication -Connections -Representation	-Nature of Technology -Technology and Society -Technological World	-English Language Arts Standards: Science & Technical Subjects

Teaching Strategies

Step #1: Engage—Review concepts. Introduce the STEM lab. Discuss the challenge presented in the lab, providing students with an opportunity to connect previous knowledge to the problem they are to solve.

Step #2: Investigate—Students conduct research to gain an understanding of the major science concepts related to the topic, review possible solutions to the lab challenge, and formulate new ideas for solving the problem.

Step #3: Explore—Students apply research to design and test a model, process, or system to solve the problem presented in the challenge.

Step #4: Communicate—Students share results.

Step #5: Evaluate—Students are given an opportunity to reflect on what they have learned.

Managing the Lab

- Set a deadline for project submission and presentations.
- Group students into collaborative teams and assign roles.
- Review prerequisite skills students need for doing the lab, such as measuring, weighing, constructing, recording data, graphing, and so on.
- Review science safety rules.
- Review lab cleanup procedures.
- Have the needed materials available, organized, and set up for easy access.
- Monitor teams and provide productive feedback.
- Leave enough time at the end of class for cleanup and debriefing.
- Designate area for project storage.

Evaluation

Student Reflection: Students think about their team's choices for the design of the prototype. Students individually complete the "Reflection" handout.

Student Self-Evaluation: Students think about their behavior and performance as a team member. Students individually complete the "Self-Evaluation Rubric."

Lab Evaluation: The teacher completes the "Lab Challenge Rubric" for each team member.

Conference: Teacher/student conferences are held to discuss the completed evaluations.

Enteric-Coated Pills: Student Challenge

STEM Lab Challenge: Design an enteric-coated pill. The pill must withstand the acidic environment of the human stomach for 10 minutes.

You Should Know
Scientists have developed a specialty covering for pills and tablets called **enteric coating**. The coating does not dissolve until after the pill has passed through the stomach and into the small intestine. The term *enteric* means "of or relating to the small intestine." This prevents stomach pain while still allowing the medication to get into our bodies.

Vocabulary Review
- matter
- pH
- acids and bases
- enteric coating

Materials You May Need
- flour
- cornstarch
- sugar
- vegetable oil
- paper plates
- plastic cups
- 32 oz. bottle with clear soda (stomach simulator)
- measuring spoons
- color-coated candy (pill)

Challenge Requirements
1. Research: Write a one- to two-page paper summarizing your research on the human digestive system, acids and bases, and enteric coating. Cite your sources. Your paper may include two pictures.
2. Model: Label a drawing of your enteric-coating process and explain your strategy.
3. Results: Record, analyze, and interpret test results.
4. Conclusion: Summarize the lab and what actually happened. It should include the purpose, a brief description of the test procedure, and explanation of results.
5. Reflection: Think about your team's choices for the enteric coating. Then complete the "Reflection" handout.
6. Evaluation: Think about your behavior and performance as a team member. Then complete the "Self-Evaluation Rubric."

Steps to Follow
Work with a team to complete the steps listed below. A team will have 3 or 4 members.

Step 1: Research the human digestive system, acids and bases, and enteric coating.
Step 2: Brainstorm ideas about a recipe for the enteric coating.
Step 3: Draw a diagram of your coating process.
Step 4: Create the enteric coating.
Step 5: Test the coating.
Step 6: Evaluate the performance of your coating.
Step 7: Identify how to improve your recipe for the enteric coating.
Step 8: Make the needed changes.
Step 9: Retest and reevaluate the improved coating.
Step 10: Share the results.

Keep it Fresh: Teacher Information

STEM Lab Overview

Students are challenged to design packaging for a food that they would find in the produce aisle at the supermarket. The packaging must keep the food clean and protect against or aid in the physical and chemical changes that occur with the food.

Concepts

- Chemical properties of matter
- Chemical changes of matter

Standards for Grades 6–8

NGSS	NCTM	ITEA	CCSS
-Structure and Properties of Matter	-Problem Solving -Communication -Connections -Representation	-Nature of Technology -Technology and Society -Technological World	-English Language Arts Standards: Science & Technical Subjects

Teaching Strategies

Step #1: Engage—Review concepts. Introduce the STEM lab. Discuss the challenge presented in the lab, providing students with an opportunity to connect previous knowledge to the problem they are to solve.

Step #2: Investigate—Students conduct research to gain an understanding of the major science concepts related to the topic, review possible solutions to the lab challenge, and formulate new ideas for solving the problem.

Step #3: Explore—Students apply research to design and test a model, process, or system to solve the problem presented in the challenge.

Step #4: Communicate—Students share results.

Step #5: Evaluate—Students are given an opportunity to reflect on what they have learned.

Managing the Lab

- Set a deadline for project submission and presentations.
- Group students into collaborative teams and assign roles.
- Review prerequisite skills students need for doing the lab, such as measuring, weighing, constructing, recording data, graphing, and so on.
- Review science safety rules.
- Review lab cleanup procedures.
- Have the needed materials available, organized, and set up for easy access.
- Monitor teams and provide productive feedback.
- Leave enough time at the end of class for cleanup and debriefing.
- Designate area for project storage.

Evaluation

Student Reflection: Students think about their team's choices for the design of the prototype. Students individually complete the "Reflection" handout.

Student Self-Evaluation: Students think about their behavior and performance as a team member. Students individually complete the "Self-Evaluation Rubric."

Lab Evaluation: The teacher completes the "Lab Challenge Rubric" for each team member.

Conference: Teacher/student conferences are held to discuss the completed evaluations.

Keep it Fresh: Student Challenge

STEM Lab Challenge: Design packaging for a food that you would find in the produce aisle at the supermarket. The packaging must keep the food clean and protect against or aid in the physical and chemical changes that occur with the food.

You Should Know

Packaging is a huge, profitable industry; often it is the way the packaging looks that persuades the shopper to buy the product inside. Foods are packaged to protect and preserve the product for as long as possible.

Vocabulary Review
- chemical changes in matter
- decay
- perishable

Materials You May Need
- design materials: to be determined by student research

Challenge Requirements

1. <u>Research</u>: Write a one- to two-page paper summarizing your research on food packaging and package engineering. Cite your sources. Your paper may include two pictures.
2. <u>Model</u>: Label a drawing of your package design and explain your strategy.
3. <u>Results</u>: Record, analyze, and interpret test results.
4. <u>Conclusion</u>: Summarize the lab and what actually happened. It should include the purpose, a brief description of the test procedure, and explanation of results.
5. <u>Reflection</u>: Think about your team's choices for the package design. Then complete the "Reflection" handout.
6. <u>Evaluation</u>: Think about your behavior and performance as a team member. Then complete the "Self-Evaluation Rubric."

Steps to Follow

Work with a team to complete the steps listed below. A team will have 3 or 4 members.

Step 1: Research food packaging and package engineering.
Step 2: Brainstorm ideas about how to design a package to meet the requirements of the lab. Consider moisture, light, and temperature when designing your packaging.
Step 3: Draw a diagram of your design.
Step 4: Create the package.
Step 5: Test the package.
Step 6: Evaluate the performance of your package.
Step 7: Identify how to improve your package.
Step 8: Make the needed changes.
Step 9: Retest and reevaluate the improved design.
Step 10: Share the results.

Chemical Compound Model: Teacher Information

STEM Lab Overview

Students are challenged to design a three-dimensional model that demonstrates how atoms bond in a chemical compound.

Concepts

- Elements, molecules, and compounds
- Chemical bonds

Standards for Grades 6–8

NGSS	NCTM	ITEA	CCSS
-Structure and Properties of Matter	-Problem Solving -Communication -Connections -Representation	-Nature of Technology -Technology and Society -Technological World	-English Language Arts Standards: Science & Technical Subjects

Teaching Strategies

Step #1: Engage—Review concepts. Introduce the STEM lab. Discuss the challenge presented in the lab, providing students with an opportunity to connect previous knowledge to the problem they are to solve.

Step #2: Investigate—Students conduct research to gain an understanding of the major science concepts related to the topic, review possible solutions to the lab challenge, and formulate new ideas for solving the problem.

Step #3: Explore—Students apply research to design and test a model, process, or system to solve the problem presented in the challenge.

Step #4: Communicate—Students share results.

Step #5: Evaluate—Students are given an opportunity to reflect on what they have learned.

Managing the Lab

- Set a deadline for project submission and presentations.
- Group students into collaborative teams and assign roles.
- Review prerequisite skills students need for doing the lab, such as measuring, weighing, constructing, recording data, graphing, and so on.
- Review science safety rules.
- Review lab cleanup procedures.
- Have the needed materials available, organized, and set up for easy access.
- Monitor teams and provide productive feedback.
- Leave enough time at the end of class for cleanup and debriefing.
- Designate area for project storage.

Evaluation

Student Reflection: Students think about their team's choices for the design of the prototype. Students individually complete the "Reflection" handout.

Student Self-Evaluation: Students think about their behavior and performance as a team member. Students individually complete the "Self-Evaluation Rubric."

Lab Evaluation: The teacher completes the "Lab Challenge Rubric" for each team member.

Conference: Teacher/student conferences are held to discuss the completed evaluations.

Chemical Compound Model: Student Challenge

STEM Lab Challenge: Design a three-dimensional model that demonstrates how atoms bond in a compound.

You Should Know

All matter is made up of atoms. Different kinds of atoms are called elements. Two or more elements that have combined are called a compound. The elements in a compound are held together by chemical bonds. Two types of chemical bonds are ionic bonds and covalent bonds.

Vocabulary Review

- atom
- chemical bond
- compound
- covalent bond
- element
- electron
- ionic bond
- molecules

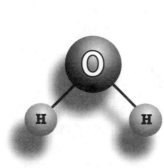

Materials You May Need

- design materials: to be determined by student research

Steps to Follow

Work with a team to complete the steps listed below. A team will have 3 or 4 members.

Step 1: Research compounds and chemical bonds.

Step 2: Choose a compound and brainstorm ideas about the materials to use in the design of your compound. Think about how to show the difference between the atoms of the various elements in the compound and the correct number of bonds each atom forms.

Step 3: Draw a diagram of your design.

Step 4: Construct the model.

Step 5: Test the model.

Step 6: Test the accuracy of your model by using your science book or other resources. Record the results of your comparison.

Step 7: Identify how to improve the design of your model.

Step 8: Make the needed changes.

Step 9: Retest and reevaluate the improved design.

Step 10: Share the results.

Challenge Requirements

1. <u>Research</u>: Write a one- to two-page paper summarizing your research on compounds and chemical bonds. Cite your sources. Your paper may include two pictures.
2. <u>Model</u>: Label a drawing of your compound design and explain your strategy.
3. <u>Results</u>: Record, analyze, and interpret test results.
4. <u>Conclusion</u>: Summarize the task and what actually happened. It should include the purpose, a brief description of the test procedure, and explanation of results.
5. <u>Reflection</u>: Think about your team's choices for the compound design. Then complete the "Reflection" handout.
6. <u>Evaluation</u>: Think about your behavior and performance as a team member. Then complete the "Self-Evaluation Rubric."

Save That Ice!: Teacher Information

STEM Lab Overview
Students are challenged to design a shoebox-size device that keeps three ice cubes from melting under a heat lamp for 30 minutes.

Concepts
• Properties of matter   • States of matter   • Insulation   • Refrigeration

Standards for Grades 6–8

NGSS	NCTM	ITEA	CCSS
-Structure and Properties of Matter -Energy	-Problem Solving -Communication -Connections -Representation	-Nature of Technology -Technology and Society -Technological World	-English Language Arts Standards: Science & Technical Subjects

Teaching Strategies

Step #1: Engage—Review concepts. Introduce the STEM lab. Discuss the challenge presented in the lab, providing students with an opportunity to connect previous knowledge to the problem they are to solve.

Step #2: Investigate—Students conduct research to gain an understanding of the major science concepts related to the topic, review possible solutions to the lab challenge, and formulate new ideas for solving the problem.

Step #3: Explore—Students apply research to design and test a model, process, or system to solve the problem presented in the challenge.

Step #4: Communicate—Students share results.

Step #5: Evaluate—Students are given an opportunity to reflect on what they have learned.

Managing the Lab

• Set a deadline for project submission and presentations.
• Group students into collaborative teams and assign roles.
• Review prerequisite skills students need for doing the lab, such as measuring, weighing, constructing, recording data, graphing, and so on.
• Review science safety rules.
• Review lab cleanup procedures.
• Have the needed materials available, organized, and set up for easy access.
• Monitor teams and provide productive feedback.
• Leave enough time at the end of class for cleanup and debriefing.
• Designate area for project storage.

Evaluation

Student Reflection: Students think about their team's choices for the design of the prototype. Students individually complete the "Reflection" handout.

Student Self-Evaluation: Students think about their behavior and performance as a team member. Students individually complete the "Self-Evaluation Rubric."

Lab Evaluation: The teacher completes the "Lab Challenge Rubric" for each team member.

Conference: Teacher/student conferences are held to discuss the completed evaluations.

Save That Ice!: Student Challenge

STEM Lab Challenge: Design a shoebox-size device that keeps three ice cubes from melting under a heat lamp for 30 minutes.

You Should Know

Before the invention of refrigerators, ice was stored in icehouses. Some were man-made underground chambers, while many were buildings with various types of insulation.

Vocabulary Review

- heat
- heat transfer
- insulation
- matter
- melting point
- temperature

Materials You May Need

- heat lamp
- timer
- ice cubes
- cardboard box or shoebox
- masking tape
- other design materials: to be determined by student research

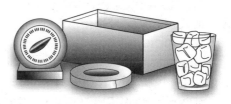

Challenge Requirements

1. <u>Research</u>: Write a one- to two-page paper summarizing your research on insulation and refrigeration. Cite your sources. Your paper may include two pictures.
2. <u>Model</u>: Label a drawing of your device design and explain your strategy.
3. <u>Results</u>: Record, analyze, and interpret test results.
4. <u>Conclusion</u>: Summarize the lab and what actually happened. It should include the purpose, a brief description of the test procedure, and explanation of results.
5. <u>Reflection</u>: Think about your team's choices for the device design. Then complete the "Reflection" handout.
6. <u>Evaluation</u>: Think about your behavior and performance as a team member. Then complete the "Self-Evaluation Rubric."

Steps to Follow

Work with a team to complete the steps listed below. A team will have 3 or 4 members.

Step 1: Research insulation and refrigeration.
Step 2: Brainstorm ideas about how to design a device to meet the requirements of the lab. Think about how you will test your design.
Step 3: Draw a diagram of your design.
Step 4: Construct the device.
Step 5: Test the device.
Step 6: Evaluate the performance of your design.
Step 7: Identify how to improve the design of your device.
Step 8: Make the needed changes.
Step 9: Retest and reevaluate the improved design.
Step 10: Share the results.

The Hydrophobic Effect: Teacher Information

STEM Lab Overview

Students are challenged to design a process for waterproofing a piece of cotton fabric. The water should not be absorbed by the fabric but should bead up on the surface of the fabric instead.

Concepts

- Surface tension
- Hydrophobic effect

Standards for Grades 6–8

NGSS	NCTM	ITEA	CCSS
-Structure and Properties of Matter	-Problem Solving -Communication -Connections -Representation	-Nature of Technology -Technology and Society -Technological World	-English Language Arts Standards: Science & Technical Subjects

Teaching Strategies

Step #1: Engage—Review concepts. Introduce the STEM lab. Discuss the challenge presented in the lab, providing students with an opportunity to connect previous knowledge to the problem they are to solve.

Step #2: Investigate—Students conduct research to gain an understanding of the major science concepts related to the topic, review possible solutions to the lab challenge, and formulate new ideas for solving the problem.

Step #3: Explore—Students apply research to design and test a model, process, or system to solve the problem presented in the challenge.

Step #4: Communicate—Students share results.

Step #5: Evaluate—Students are given an opportunity to reflect on what they have learned.

Managing the Lab

- Set a deadline for project submission and presentations.
- Group students into collaborative teams and assign roles.
- Review prerequisite skills students need for doing the lab, such as measuring, weighing, constructing, recording data, graphing, and so on.
- Review science safety rules.
- Review lab cleanup procedures.
- Have the needed materials available, organized, and set up for easy access.
- Monitor teams and provide productive feedback.
- Leave enough time at the end of class for cleanup and debriefing.
- Designate area for project storage.

Evaluation

Student Reflection: Students think about their team's choices for the design of the prototype. Students individually complete the "Reflection" handout.

Student Self-Evaluation: Students think about their behavior and performance as a team member. Students individually complete the "Self-Evaluation Rubric."

Lab Evaluation: The teacher completes the "Lab Challenge Rubric" for each team member.

Conference: Teacher/student conferences are held to discuss the completed evaluations.

The Hydrophobic Effect: Student Challenge

STEM Lab Challenge: Design a process for waterproofing a piece of cotton fabric. The water should not be absorbed by the fabric but should bead up on the surface instead.

You Should Know
Waterproof fabrics prevent water droplets from being absorbed. They are made by closely knitting the fibers or coating the fabric with a waterproofing substance.

Vocabulary Review
- hydrophobic effect
- polarity
- waterproof
- molecule
- surface tension

Materials You May Need
- cotton cloth, cut into 6-inch squares
- clay
- crayons
- glue
- flax seed
- lanolin
- wax
- water
- other materials: to be determined by student research

Challenge Requirements
1. <u>Research</u>: Write a one- to two-page paper summarizing your research on surface tension, the hydrophobic effect, and waterproofing. Cite your sources. Your paper may include two pictures.
2. <u>Model</u>: Label a drawing of your waterproofing process and explain your strategy.
3. <u>Results</u>: Record, analyze, and interpret test results.
4. <u>Conclusion</u>: Summarize the lab and what actually happened. It should include the purpose, a brief description of the test procedure, and explanation of results.
5. <u>Reflection</u>: Think about your team's choices for the waterproofing process. Then complete the "Reflection" handout.
6. <u>Evaluation</u>: Think about your behavior and performance as a team member. Then complete the "Self-Evaluation Rubric."

Steps to Follow
Work with a team to complete the steps listed below. A team will have 3 or 4 members.

Step 1: Research surface tension, the hydrophobic effect, and waterproofing.
Step 2: Brainstorm ideas about a process for waterproofing your cotton material to meet the requirements of the lab.
Step 3: Draw a diagram of your process.
Step 4: Create the waterproofed material.
Step 5: Test the material.
Step 6: Evaluate the performance of your waterproofed material.
Step 7: Identify how to improve your process for waterproofing.
Step 8: Make the needed changes.
Step 9: Retest and reevaluate the improved process.
Step 10: Share the results.

Bubbling Bottle Lamp: Teacher Information

STEM Lab Overview
Students are challenged to design a lava lamp using a clear plastic soda bottle.

Concepts
• Mixtures   • Solutions   • Suspensions

Standards for Grades 6–8			
NGSS	**NCTM**	**ITEA**	**CCSS**
-Structure and Properties of Matter	-Problem Solving -Communication -Connections -Representation	-Nature of Technology -Technology and Society -Technological World	-English Language Arts Standards: Science & Technical Subjects

Teaching Strategies

Step #1:   Engage—Review concepts. Introduce the STEM lab. Discuss the challenge presented in the lab, providing students with an opportunity to connect previous knowledge to the problem they are to solve.

Step #2:   Investigate—Students conduct research to gain an understanding of the major science concepts related to the topic, review possible solutions to the lab challenge, and formulate new ideas for solving the problem.

Step #3:   Explore—Students apply research to design and test a model, process, or system to solve the problem presented in the challenge.

Step #4:   Communicate—Students share results.

Step #5:   Evaluate—Students are given an opportunity to reflect on what they have learned.

Managing the Lab

• Set a deadline for project submission and presentations.
• Group students into collaborative teams and assign roles.
• Review prerequisite skills students need for doing the lab, such as measuring, weighing, constructing, recording data, graphing, and so on.
• Review science safety rules.
• Review lab cleanup procedures.
• Have the needed materials available, organized, and set up for easy access.
• Monitor teams and provide productive feedback.
• Leave enough time at the end of class for cleanup and debriefing.
• Designate area for project storage.

Evaluation

Student Reflection: Students think about their team's choices for the design of the prototype. Students individually complete the "Reflection" handout.

Student Self-Evaluation: Students think about their behavior and performance as a team member. Students individually complete the "Self-Evaluation Rubric."

Lab Evaluation: The teacher completes the "Lab Challenge Rubric" for each team member.

Conference: Teacher/student conferences are held to discuss the completed evaluations.

Matter

Bubbling Bottle Lamp: Student Challenge

STEM Lab Challenge: Design a lava lamp using a clear plastic soda bottle.

You Should Know

Edward Craven-Walker invented the lava lamp in 1963. He got his inspiration after watching a homemade egg timer bubbling on a stove top.

Vocabulary Review

- compound
- element
- mixture
- solute
- solution
- solvent
- suspension

Materials You May Need

- an assortment of clear plastic soda bottles
- food coloring
- inexpensive vegetable oil
- water
- effervescing antacid tablet
- flashlight

Challenge Requirements

1. <u>Research</u>: Write a one- to two-page paper summarizing your research on mixtures, solutions, and suspensions. Cite your sources. Your paper may include two pictures.
2. <u>Model</u>: Label a drawing of your bottle lamp design and explain your strategy.
3. <u>Results</u>: Record, analyze, and interpret test results.
4. <u>Conclusion</u>: Summarize the lab and what actually happened. It should include the purpose, a brief description of the test procedure, and explanation of results.
5. <u>Reflection</u>: Think about your team's choices for the lamp design. Then complete the "Reflection" handout.
6. <u>Evaluation</u>: Think about your behavior and performance as a team member. Then complete the "Self-Evaluation Rubric."

Steps to Follow

Work with a team to complete the steps listed below. A team will have 3 or 4 members.

Step 1: Research mixtures, solutions, and suspensions.

Step 2: Brainstorm ideas about how to meet the requirements of the lab. Think about the materials to use in your bottle lamp design.

Step 3: Draw a diagram of your design.

Step 4: Construct the lamp.

Step 5: Test the lamp.

Step 6: Evaluate the performance of your bottle lamp design.

Step 7: Identify how to improve the performance of your lamp.

Step 8: Make the needed changes.

Step 9: Retest and reevaluate the improved design.

Step 10: Share the results.

Measuring Mass: Teacher Information

STEM Lab Overview

Students are challenged to design a device to accurately measure the mass of solids. The device should be accurate to 0.5 grams.

Concepts

- International System (SI) of measurement   • Mass

Standards for Grades 6–8

NGSS	NCTM	ITEA	CCSS
-Structure and Properties of Matter	-Problem Solving -Communication -Connections -Representation	-Nature of Technology -Technology and Society -Technological World	-English Language Arts Standards: Science & Technical Subjects

Teaching Strategies

Step #1: Engage—Review concepts. Introduce the STEM lab. Discuss the challenge presented in the lab, providing students with an opportunity to connect previous knowledge to the problem they are to solve.

Step #2: Investigate—Students conduct research to gain an understanding of the major science concepts related to the topic, review possible solutions to the lab challenge, and formulate new ideas for solving the problem.

Step #3: Explore—Students apply research to design and test a model, process, or system to solve the problem presented in the challenge.

Step #4: Communicate—Students share results.

Step #5: Evaluate—Students are given an opportunity to reflect on what they have learned.

Managing the Lab

- Set a deadline for project submission and presentations.
- Group students into collaborative teams and assign roles.
- Review prerequisite skills students need for doing the lab, such as measuring, weighing, constructing, recording data, graphing, and so on.
- Review science safety rules.
- Review lab cleanup procedures.
- Have the needed materials available, organized, and set up for easy access.
- Monitor teams and provide productive feedback.
- Leave enough time at the end of class for cleanup and debriefing.
- Designate area for project storage.

Evaluation

Student Reflection: Students think about their team's choices for the design of the prototype. Students individually complete the "Reflection" handout.

Student Self-Evaluation: Students think about their behavior and performance as a team member. Students individually complete the "Self-Evaluation Rubric."

Lab Evaluation: The teacher completes the "Lab Challenge Rubric" for each team member.

Conference: Teacher/student conferences are held to discuss the completed evaluations.

Measuring Mass: Student Challenge

STEM Lab Challenge: Design a device to accurately measure the mass of solids. The device should be accurate to 0.5 grams.

You Should Know

Scientists all over the world use an accepted system of standard measurements so they can communicate their research and lab results without confusion. The International System of Units (SI), commonly known as the metric system, is the international standard scientists use for measurement.

Vocabulary Review

- balance scale
- gram
- International System (SI) of measurement
- mass
- metric system
- measurement

Materials You May Need

- weights for measuring mass
- electronic balance
- plastic, Styrofoam, and paper cups
- ruler, yardstick, wooden dowel, and 10-gallon paint stick
- metal and plastic clothes hangers
- different styles of paper clips
- string and tape
- objects to measure
- other design materials: to be determined by student research

Challenge Requirements

1. <u>Research</u>: Write a one- to two-page paper summarizing your research on mass, balance scale, and International System (SI) of measurement. Cite your sources. Your paper may include two pictures.
2. <u>Model</u>: Label a drawing of your device and explain your strategy.
3. <u>Results</u>: Record, analyze, and interpret test results.
4. <u>Conclusion</u>: Summarize the lab and what actually happened. It should include the purpose, a brief description of the test procedure, and explanation of results.
5. <u>Reflection</u>: Think about your team's choices for the device. Then complete the "Reflection" handout.
6. <u>Evaluation</u>: Think about your behavior and performance as a team member. Then complete the "Self-Evaluation Rubric."

Steps to Follow

Work with a team to complete the steps listed below. A team will have 3 or 4 members.

Step 1: Research mass, states of matter, balance scale, and International System (SI) of measurement.
Step 2: Brainstorm ideas about how to design a device for measuring mass to meet the requirements of the lab. Think about how you will test the accuracy of your device.
Step 3: Draw a diagram of your design.
Step 4: Construct the measuring device.
Step 5: Test the device.
Step 6: Evaluate the performance of your measuring device.
Step 7: Identify how to improve the design of your device.
Step 8: Make the needed changes.
Step 9: Retest and reevaluate the improved design.
Step 10: Share the results.

Vending Machine Drop: Teacher Information

STEM Lab Overview

Students are challenged to design a package that is sturdy, inexpensive, and environmentally friendly that will protect a cookie when dropped from a distance of 1.5 meters from the top shelf of a vending machine.

Concepts

- Newton's First Law of Motion

Standards for Grades 6–8

NGSS	NCTM	ITEA	CCSS
-Force and Interactions	-Problem Solving -Communication -Connections -Representation	-Nature of Technology -Technology and Society -Technological World	-English Language Arts Standards: Science & Technical Subjects

Teaching Strategies

Step #1: Engage—Review concepts. Introduce the STEM lab. Discuss the challenge presented in the lab, providing students with an opportunity to connect previous knowledge to the problem they are to solve.

Step #2: Investigate—Students conduct research to gain an understanding of the major science concepts related to the topic, review possible solutions to the lab challenge, and formulate new ideas for solving the problem.

Step #3: Explore—Students apply research to design and test a model, process, or system to solve the problem presented in the challenge.

Step #4: Communicate—Students share results.

Step #5: Evaluate—Students are given an opportunity to reflect on what they have learned.

Managing the Lab

- Set a deadline for project submission and presentations.
- Group students into collaborative teams and assign roles.
- Review prerequisite skills students need for doing the lab, such as measuring, weighing, constructing, recording data, graphing, and so on.
- Review science safety rules.
- Review lab cleanup procedures.
- Have the needed materials available, organized, and set up for easy access.
- Monitor teams and provide productive feedback.
- Leave enough time at the end of class for cleanup and debriefing.
- Designate area for project storage.

Evaluation

Student Reflection: Students think about their team's choices for the design of the prototype. Students individually complete the "Reflection" handout.

Student Self-Evaluation: Students think about their behavior and performance as a team member. Students individually complete the "Self-Evaluation Rubric."

Lab Evaluation: The teacher completes the "Lab Challenge Rubric" for each team member.

Conference: Teacher/student conferences are held to discuss the completed evaluations.

Vending Machine Drop: Student Challenge

STEM Lab Challenge: Design a package that is sturdy, inexpensive, and environmentally friendly that will protect a cookie when dropped from a distance of 1.5 meters off the top shelf of a vending machine.

You Should Know

With a touch of a button, a vending machine dispenses just about every type of food you can imagine. They have brought a great deal of convenience to our lives. Vending machines and the quality of food inside them is a constantly evolving industry.

Vocabulary Review

- Newton's First Law of Motion
- inertia
- motion
- velocity
- speed
- acceleration
- gravity

Materials You May Need

- variety of cookies
- meter stick
- package design materials: to be determined by student research

Challenge Requirements

1. <u>Research</u>: Write a one- to two-page paper summarizing your research on snack food packaging and Newton's First Law of Motion. Cite your sources. Your paper may include two pictures.
2. <u>Model</u>: Label a drawing of your package design and explain your strategy.
3. <u>Results</u>: Record, analyze, and interpret test results.
4. <u>Conclusion</u>: Summarize the lab and what actually happened. It should include the purpose, a brief description of the test procedure, and explanation of results.
5. <u>Reflection</u>: Think about your team's choices for the package design. Then complete the "Reflection" handout.
6. <u>Evaluation</u>: Think about your behavior and performance as a team member. Then complete the "Self-Evaluation Rubric."

Steps to Follow

Work with a team to complete the steps listed below. A team will have 3 or 4 members.

Step 1: Research snack food packaging and Newton's First Law of Motion.
Step 2: Brainstorm ideas about how to design a package to meet the requirements of the lab. Think about how you will test your design.
Step 3: Draw a diagram of your design.
Step 4: Create the package.
Step 5: Test the package.
Step 6: Evaluate the performance of your design.
Step 7: Identify how to improve the design of your package.
Step 8: Make the needed changes.
Step 9: Retest and reevaluate the improved design.
Step 10: Share the results.

Bridge Building: Teacher Information

STEM Lab Overview

Students are challenged to design a bridge that will span a distance of at least 35 centimeters. The bridge must hold 10 pounds for 5 minutes when placed 1 meter above the floor.

Concepts to Review

• Bridge structures	• Bridge design	• Newton's First and Third Laws of Motion

Standards for Grades 6–8

NGSS	NCTM	ITEA	CCSS
-Force and Interactions	-Problem Solving -Communication -Connections -Representation	-Nature of Technology -Technology and Society -Technological World	-English Language Arts Standards: Science & Technical Subjects

Teaching Strategies

Step #1: Engage—Review concepts. Introduce the STEM lab. Discuss the challenge presented in the lab, providing students with an opportunity to connect previous knowledge to the problem they are to solve.

Step #2: Investigate—Students conduct research to gain an understanding of the major science concepts related to the topic, review possible solutions to the lab challenge, and formulate new ideas for solving the problem.

Step #3: Explore—Students apply research to design and test a model, process, or system to solve the problem presented in the challenge.

Step #4: Communicate—Students share results.

Step #5: Evaluate—Students are given an opportunity to reflect on what they have learned.

Managing the Lab

- Set a deadline for project submission and presentations.
- Group students into collaborative teams and assign roles.
- Review prerequisite skills students need for doing the lab, such as measuring, weighing, constructing, recording data, graphing, and so on.
- Review science safety rules.
- Review lab cleanup procedures.
- Have the needed materials available, organized, and set up for easy access.
- Monitor teams and provide productive feedback.
- Leave enough time at the end of class for cleanup and debriefing.
- Designate area for project storage.

Evaluation

<u>Student Reflection</u>: Students think about their team's choices for the design of the prototype. Students individually complete the "Reflection" handout.

<u>Student Self-Evaluation</u>: Students think about their behavior and performance as a team member. Students individually complete the "Self-Evaluation Rubric."

<u>Lab Evaluation</u>: The teacher completes the "Lab Challenge Rubric" for each team member.

<u>Conference</u>: Teacher/student conferences are held to discuss the completed evaluations.

Bridge Building: Student Challenge

STEM Lab Challenge: Design a bridge that will span a distance of at least 35 centimeters. The bridge must hold 10 pounds for 5 minutes when placed 1 meter above the floor.

You Should Know

There are six main types of bridges: arch, beam, cable-stayed, cantilever, suspension, and truss.

Arch   Beam   Cable-stayed

Cantilever   Suspension   Truss

Vocabulary Review
- action/reaction forces
- balanced/unbalanced forces
- beam
- bridge
- compression forces
- load
- span
- truss

Materials You May Need
- meter stick
- 200 popsicle sticks
- wood glue
- clamps
- testing materials: sand, bucket with bale, rope, twine, triple-beam balance

Challenge Requirements

1. <u>Research</u>: Write a one- to two-page paper summarizing your research on bridges and bridge engineering. Cite your sources. Your paper may include two pictures.
2. <u>Model</u>: Label a drawing of your bridge design and explain your strategy.
3. <u>Results</u>: Record, analyze, and interpret test results.
4. <u>Conclusion</u>: Summarize the lab and what actually happened. It should include the purpose, a brief description of the test procedure, and explanation of results.
5. <u>Reflection</u>: Think about your team's choices for the bridge design. Then complete the "Reflection" handout.
6. <u>Evaluation</u>: Think about your behavior and performance as a team member. Then complete the "Self-Evaluation Rubric."

Steps to Follow

Work with a team to complete the steps listed below. A team will have 3 or 4 members.

Step 1: Research bridges and bridge engineering.

Step 2: Brainstorm ideas about how to design a bridge to meet the requirements of the lab. Think about how you will test your design.

Step 3: Draw a diagram of your design.

Step 4: Construct the bridge.

Step 5: Test the bridge.

Step 6: Evaluate the performance of your design.

Step 7: Identify how to improve the design of your bridge.

Step 8: Make the needed changes.

Step 9: Retest and reevaluate the improved design.

Step 10: Share the results.

Furniture Fun: Teacher Information

STEM Lab Overview

Students are challenged to design a chair made entirely of cardboard and glue. The chair must have a seat and sturdy back; it should comfortably support the weight of a team member.

Concepts

- Ergonomics
- Force
- Gravity

Standards for Grades 6–8

NGSS	NCTM	ITEA	CCSS
-Force and Interactions	-Problem Solving -Communication -Connections -Representation	-Nature of Technology -Technology and Society -Technological World	-English Language Arts Standards: Science & Technical Subjects

Teaching Strategies

Step #1: Engage—Review concepts. Introduce the STEM lab. Discuss the challenge presented in the lab, providing students with an opportunity to connect previous knowledge to the problem they are to solve.

Step #2: Investigate—Students conduct research to gain an understanding of the major science concepts related to the topic, review possible solutions to the lab challenge, and formulate new ideas for solving the problem.

Step #3: Explore—Students apply research to design and test a model, process, or system to solve the problem presented in the challenge.

Step #4: Communicate—Students share results.

Step #5: Evaluate—Students are given an opportunity to reflect on what they have learned.

Managing the Lab

- Set a deadline for project submission and presentations.
- Group students into collaborative teams and assign roles.
- Review prerequisite skills students need for doing the lab, such as measuring, weighing, constructing, recording data, graphing, and so on.
- Review science safety rules.
- Review lab cleanup procedures.
- Have the needed materials available, organized, and set up for easy access.
- Monitor teams and provide productive feedback.
- Leave enough time at the end of class for cleanup and debriefing.
- Designate area for project storage.

Evaluation

Student Reflection: Students think about their team's choices for the design of the prototype. Students individually complete the "Reflection" handout.

Student Self-Evaluation: Students think about their behavior and performance as a team member. Students individually complete the "Self-Evaluation Rubric."

Lab Evaluation: The teacher completes the "Lab Challenge Rubric" for each team member.

Conference: Teacher/student conferences are held to discuss the completed evaluations.

Furniture Fun: Student Challenge

STEM Lab Challenge: Design and construct a chair made entirely of cardboard and glue. The chair must have a seat and sturdy back; it should comfortably support the weight of a team member.

You Should Know

Cardboard is a durable material made of paper and wood pulp. Many people are now choosing to use heavy cardboard for furniture because of its versatility and environmental friendliness. Custom-made cardboard furniture can take on just about any shape imaginable.

Vocabulary Review

- center of gravity
- compression
- ergonomics
- force
- load
- mass

Materials You May Need

- glue
- various cardboard material: to be determined through student research

Challenge Requirements

1. <u>Research</u>: Write a one- to two-page paper summarizing your research on ergonomics and cardboard furniture. Cite your sources. Your paper may include two pictures.
2. <u>Model</u>: Label a drawing of your chair design and explain your strategy.
3. <u>Results</u>: Record, analyze, and interpret test results.
4. <u>Conclusion</u>: Summarize the lab and what actually happened. It should include the purpose, a brief description of the test procedure, and explanation of results.
5. <u>Reflection</u>: Think about your team's choices for the chair design. Then complete the "Reflection" handout.
6. <u>Evaluation</u>: Think about your behavior and performance as a team member. Then complete the "Self-Evaluation Rubric."

Steps to Follow

Work with a team to complete the steps listed below. A team will have 3 or 4 members.

Step 1:   Research ergonomics and cardboard furniture.
Step 2:   Brainstorm ideas about how to design a cardboard chair to meet the requirements of the lab. Think about the kind of glue you will use to assemble your chair.
Step 3:   Draw a diagram of your chair design.
Step 4:   Construct the chair.
Step 5:   Test the chair.
Step 6:   Evaluate the performance of your design.
Step 7:   Identify how to improve the design of your chair.
Step 8:   Make the needed changes.
Step 9:   Retest and reevaluate the improved design.
Step 10: Share the results.

Forces and Motion

Zip Line Ride: Teacher Information

STEM Lab Overview

Students are challenged to design a gondola that can zip down a line and drop a marble onto a target.

Concepts

- Newton's Laws of Motion   • Energy transfer

Standards for Grades 6–8

NGSS	NCTM	ITEA	CCSS
-Force and Interactions -Energy	-Problem Solving -Communication -Connections -Representation	-Nature of Technology -Technology and Society -Technological World	-English Language Arts Standards: Science & Technical Subjects

Teaching Strategies

Step #1: Engage—Review concepts. Introduce the STEM lab. Discuss the challenge presented in the lab, providing students with an opportunity to connect previous knowledge to the problem they are to solve.

Step #2: Investigate—Students conduct research to gain an understanding of the major science concepts related to the topic, review possible solutions to the lab challenge, and formulate new ideas for solving the problem.

Step #3: Explore—Students apply research to design and test a model, process, or system to solve the problem presented in the challenge.

Step #4: Communicate—Students share results.

Step #5: Evaluate—Students are given an opportunity to reflect on what they have learned.

Managing the Lab

- Set a deadline for project submission and presentations.
- Group students into collaborative teams and assign roles.
- Review prerequisite skills students need for doing the lab, such as measuring, weighing, constructing, recording data, graphing, and so on.
- Review science safety rules.
- Review lab cleanup procedures.
- Have the needed materials available, organized, and set up for easy access.
- Monitor teams and provide productive feedback.
- Leave enough time at the end of class for cleanup and debriefing.
- Designate area for project storage.

Evaluation

Student Reflection: Students think about their team's choices for the design of the prototype. Students individually complete the "Reflection" handout.

Student Self-Evaluation: Students think about their behavior and performance as a team member. Students individually complete the "Self-Evaluation Rubric."

Lab Evaluation: The teacher completes the "Lab Challenge Rubric" for each team member.

Conference: Teacher/student conferences are held to discuss the completed evaluations.

Forces and Motion

Zip Line Ride: Student Challenge

STEM Lab Challenge: Design a gondola that can zip down a line and drop a marble onto a target.

You Should Know
Zip line rides are popular outdoor activities. The ride uses gravity to get the user from the top to the bottom of an incline.

Vocabulary Review
- acceleration
- force
- friction
- gravity
- inertia
- kinetic energy
- mass
- momentum
- motion
- transfer of energy
- potential energy
- work

Materials You May Need
- an assortment of paper cups
- index cards
- kite string or fishing line
- paper clips
- marbles
- scissors
- tape
- target
- other design materials: to be determined by student research

Challenge Requirements
1. <u>Research</u>: Write a one- to two-page paper summarizing your research on zip lines and Newton's Laws of Motion. Cite your sources. Your paper may include two pictures.
2. <u>Model</u>: Label a drawing of your zip line and gondola design and explain your strategy.
3. <u>Results</u>: Record, analyze, and interpret test results.
4. <u>Conclusion</u>: Summarize the lab and what actually happened. It should include the purpose, a brief description of the test procedure, and explanation of results.
5. <u>Reflection</u>: Think about your team's choices for the zip line and gondola. Then complete the "Reflection" handout.
6. <u>Evaluation</u>: Think about your behavior and performance as a team member. Then complete the "Self-Evaluation Rubric."

Steps to Follow
Work with a team to complete the steps listed below. A team will have 3 or 4 members.

Step 1: Research zip lines and Newton's Laws of Motion.
Step 2: Brainstorm ideas about how to meet the requirements of the lab. Think about how you will design the gondola to release the marble over your target.
Step 3: Draw a diagram of your zip line and gondola design.
Step 4: Create the model.
Step 5: Test the model.
Step 6: Evaluate the performance of your zip line and gondola.
Step 7: Identify how to improve the design of your gondola.
Step 8: Make the needed changes.
Step 9: Retest and reevaluate the improved design.
Step 10: Share the results.

Big Wheel: Teacher Information

STEM Lab Overview

Students are challenged to design a Ferris wheel with passenger gondolas. The Ferris wheel should be free-standing and able to rotate.

Concepts

- Simple machines
- Newton's First and Second Laws of Motion

Standards for Grades 6–8

NGSS	NCTM	ITEA	CCSS
-Force and Interactions	-Problem Solving -Communication -Connections -Representation	-Nature of Technology -Technology and Society -Technological World	-English Language Arts Standards: Science & Technical Subjects

Teaching Strategies

Step #1: Engage—Review concepts. Introduce the STEM lab. Discuss the challenge presented in the lab, providing students with an opportunity to connect previous knowledge to the problem they are to solve.

Step #2: Investigate—Students conduct research to gain an understanding of the major science concepts related to the topic, review possible solutions to the lab challenge, and formulate new ideas for solving the problem.

Step #3: Explore—Students apply research to design and test a model, process, or system to solve the problem presented in the challenge.

Step #4: Communicate—Students share results.

Step #5: Evaluate—Students are given an opportunity to reflect on what they have learned.

Managing the Lab

- Set a deadline for project submission and presentations.
- Group students into collaborative teams and assign roles.
- Review prerequisite skills students need for doing the lab, such as measuring, weighing, constructing, recording data, graphing, and so on.
- Review science safety rules.
- Review lab cleanup procedures.
- Have the needed materials available, organized, and set up for easy access.
- Monitor teams and provide productive feedback.
- Leave enough time at the end of class for cleanup and debriefing.
- Designate area for project storage.

Evaluation

<u>Student Reflection</u>: Students think about their team's choices for the design of the prototype. Students individually complete the "Reflection" handout.

<u>Student Self-Evaluation</u>: Students think about their behavior and performance as a team member. Students individually complete the "Self-Evaluation Rubric."

<u>Lab Evaluation</u>: The teacher completes the "Lab Challenge Rubric" for each team member.

<u>Conference</u>: Teacher/student conferences are held to discuss the completed evaluations.

Forces and Motion

Big Wheel: Student Challenge

STEM Lab Challenge: Design a Ferris wheel with passenger gondolas. The Ferris wheel should be free-standing and able to rotate.

You Should Know
In 1893, the original Ferris Wheel was designed and constructed by George Washington Gale Ferris, Jr. It was 80.4 meters (264 feet) tall. Ferris built the amusement ride for the World's Columbian Exposition in Chicago, Illinois.

Vocabulary Review
- acceleration
- centripetal force
- gravity
- inertia
- mass
- Newton's First Law of Motion
- Newton's Second Law of Motion
- velocity
- wheel and axle

Materials You May Need
- design materials: to be determined by student research

Challenge Requirements
1. <u>Research</u>: Write a one- to two-page paper summarizing your research on Ferris wheels and Ferris wheel physics. Cite your sources. Your paper may include two pictures.
2. <u>Model</u>: Label a drawing of your Ferris wheel design and explain your strategy.
3. <u>Results</u>: Record, analyze, and interpret test results.
4. <u>Conclusion</u>: Summarize the lab and what actually happened. It should include the purpose, a brief description of the test procedure, and explanation of results.
5. <u>Reflection</u>: Think about your team's choices for the Ferris wheel design. Then complete the "Reflection" handout.
6. <u>Evaluation</u>: Think about your behavior and performance as a team member. Then complete the "Self-Evaluation Rubric."

Steps to Follow
Work with a team to complete the steps listed below. A team will have 3 or 4 members.

Step 1: Research Ferris wheels and Ferris wheel physics.
Step 2: Brainstorm ideas about how to design a Ferris wheel to meet the requirements of the lab. Think about the materials to use in your design.
Step 3: Draw a diagram of your design.
Step 4: Construct the Ferris wheel.
Step 5: Test the design.
Step 6: Evaluate the performance of your Ferris wheel.
Step 7: Identify how to improve your design.
Step 8: Make the needed changes.
Step 9: Retest and reevaluate the design.
Step 10: Share the results.

Forces and Motion

Make That Hoop!: Teacher Information

STEM Lab Overview

Students are challenged to design a Ping-Pong ball launcher that will make a basket.

Concepts

• First-class, second-class, and third-class levers   • Energy transfer

Standards for Grades 6–8

NGSS	NCTM	ITEA	CCSS
-Force and Interactions -Energy	-Problem Solving -Communication -Connections -Representation	-Nature of Technology -Technology and Society -Technological World	-English Language Arts Standards: Science & Technical Subjects

Teaching Strategies

Step #1: Engage—Review concepts. Introduce the STEM lab. Discuss the challenge presented in the lab, providing students with an opportunity to connect previous knowledge to the problem they are to solve.

Step #2: Investigate—Students conduct research to gain an understanding of the major science concepts related to the topic, review possible solutions to the lab challenge, and formulate new ideas for solving the problem.

Step #3: Explore—Students apply research to design and test a model, process, or system to solve the problem presented in the challenge.

Step #4: Communicate—Students share results.

Step #5: Evaluate—Students are given an opportunity to reflect on what they have learned.

Managing the Lab

• Set a deadline for project submission and presentations.
• Group students into collaborative teams and assign roles.
• Review prerequisite skills students need for doing the lab, such as measuring, weighing, constructing, recording data, graphing, and so on.
• Review science safety rules.
• Review lab cleanup procedures.
• Have the needed materials available, organized, and set up for easy access.
• Monitor teams and provide productive feedback.
• Leave enough time at the end of class for cleanup and debriefing.
• Designate area for project storage.

Evaluation

Student Reflection: Students think about their team's choices for the design of the prototype. Students individually complete the "Reflection" handout.

Student Self-Evaluation: Students think about their behavior and performance as a team member. Students individually complete the "Self-Evaluation Rubric."

Lab Evaluation: The teacher completes the "Lab Challenge Rubric" for each team member.

Conference: Teacher/student conferences are held to discuss the completed evaluations.

Forces and Motion

Make That Hoop!: Student Challenge

STEM Lab Challenge: Design a Ping-Pong ball launcher that will fling a Ping-Pong ball to make a basket.

You Should Know
Work in today's world is shared between man and machine. Technology has advanced to the level that many machines can do jobs faster and better than humans.

Vocabulary Review
- energy transfer
- force
- friction
- fulcrum
- gravity
- kinetic energy
- levers
- load
- potential energy
- work

Materials You May Need
- wastepaper basket
- Ping-Pong balls
- other design materials: to be determined by student research

Challenge Requirements
1. Research: Write a one- to two-page paper summarizing your research on catapults and levers. Cite your sources. Your paper may include two pictures.
2. Model: Label a drawing of your Ping-Pong ball launcher design and explain your strategy.
3. Results: Record, analyze, and interpret test results.
4. Conclusion: Summarize the lab and what actually happened. It should include the purpose, a brief description of the test procedure, and explanation of results.
5. Reflection: Think about your team's choices for the design of the Ping-Pong ball launcher. Then complete the "Reflection" handout.
6. Evaluation: Think about your behavior and performance as a team member. Then complete the "Self-Evaluation Rubric."

Steps to Follow
Work with a team to complete the steps listed below. A team will have 3 or 4 members.

Step 1: Research catapults and levers.
Step 2: Brainstorm ideas about how to design your Ping-Pong ball launcher to meet the requirements of the lab. Think about the materials to use in your design.
Step 3: Draw a diagram of your launcher design.
Step 4: Construct the launcher.
Step 5: Test the design.
Step 6: Evaluate the performance of your Ping-Pong ball launcher.
Step 7: Identify how to improve the design of your launcher.
Step 8: Make the needed changes.
Step 9: Retest and reevaluate the improved design.
Step 10: Share the results.

Iceberg Science: Teacher Information

STEM Lab Overview

Students are challenged to design an iceberg that will float with at least 80% of its surface area under water.

Concepts

- Archimedes' Principle   • Buoyancy

Standards for Grades 6–8

NGSS	NCTM	ITEA	CCSS
-Force and Interactions	-Problem Solving -Communication -Connections -Representation	-Nature of Technology -Technology and Society -Technological World	-English Language Arts Standards: Science & Technical Subjects

Teaching Strategies

Step #1: Engage—Review concepts. Introduce the STEM lab. Discuss the challenge presented in the lab, providing students with an opportunity to connect previous knowledge to the problem they are to solve.

Step #2: Investigate—Students conduct research to gain an understanding of the major science concepts related to the topic, review possible solutions to the lab challenge, and formulate new ideas for solving the problem.

Step #3: Explore—Students apply research to design and test a model, process, or system to solve the problem presented in the challenge.

Step #4: Communicate—Students share results.

Step #5: Evaluate—Students are given an opportunity to reflect on what they have learned.

Managing the Lab

- Set a deadline for project submission and presentations.
- Group students into collaborative teams and assign roles.
- Review prerequisite skills students need for doing the lab, such as measuring, weighing, constructing, recording data, graphing, and so on.
- Review science safety rules.
- Review lab cleanup procedures.
- Have the needed materials available, organized, and set up for easy access.
- Monitor teams and provide productive feedback.
- Leave enough time at the end of class for cleanup and debriefing.
- Designate area for project storage.

Evaluation

Student Reflection: Students think about their team's choices for the design of the prototype. Students individually complete the "Reflection" handout.

Student Self-Evaluation: Students think about their behavior and performance as a team member. Students individually complete the "Self-Evaluation Rubric."

Lab Evaluation: The teacher completes the "Lab Challenge Rubric" for each team member.

Conference: Teacher/student conferences are held to discuss the completed evaluations.

Iceberg Science: Student Challenge

STEM Lab Challenge: Design an iceberg that will float with at least 80% of its surface area under water.

You Should Know
The luxury steamship RMS *Titanic* hit an iceberg and sank in the North Atlantic in 1912. More than 1,500 people lost their lives as the ship plunged two miles to the ocean floor.

Vocabulary Review
- Archimedes' Principle
- fluid
- buoyancy
- displacement
- density

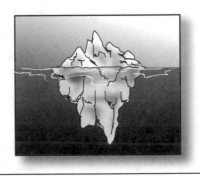

Materials You May Need
- water
- salt
- freezer
- plastic resealable freezer bags
- scissors
- ruler
- clear aquarium
- graph paper

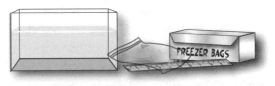

Challenge Requirements
1. <u>Research</u>: Write a one- to two-page paper summarizing your research on icebergs and Archimedes' Principle. Cite your sources. Your paper may include two pictures.
2. <u>Model</u>: Label a drawing of your model and explain your strategy.
3. <u>Results</u>: Record, analyze, and interpret test results.
4. <u>Conclusion</u>: Summarize the lab and what actually happened. It should include the purpose, a brief description of the test procedure, and explanation of results.
5. <u>Reflection</u>: Think about your team's choices for the iceberg model. Then complete the "Reflection" handout.
6. <u>Evaluation</u>: Think about your behavior and performance as a team member. Then complete the "Self-Evaluation Rubric."

Steps to Follow
Work with a team to complete the steps listed below. A team will have 3 or 4 members.

Step 1: Research icebergs and Archimedes' Principle.
Step 2: Brainstorm ideas about how to design an iceberg to meet the requirements of the lab. Think how you will determine what percent of the iceberg is below the water line.
Step 3: Draw a diagram of your design.
Step 4: Create the iceberg model.
Step 5: Test the model.
Step 6: Evaluate the performance of your iceberg model.
Step 7: Identify how to improve your design.
Step 8: Make the needed changes.
Step 9: Retest and reevaluate the model.
Step 10: Share the results.

Forces and Motion

3-D Pop Ups: Teacher Information

STEM Lab Overview

Students are challenged to design a pop-up card that incorporates origami.

Concepts

- Simple machines
- Levers

Standards for Grades 6–8

NGSS	NCTM	ITEA	CCSS
-Force and Interactions	-Problem Solving -Communication -Connections -Representation	-Nature of Technology -Technology and Society -Technological World	-English Language Arts Standards: Science & Technical Subjects

Teaching Strategies

Step #1: Engage—Review concepts. Introduce the STEM lab. Discuss the challenge presented in the lab, providing students with an opportunity to connect previous knowledge to the problem they are to solve.

Step #2: Investigate—Students conduct research to gain an understanding of the major science concepts related to the topic, review possible solutions to the lab challenge, and formulate new ideas for solving the problem.

Step #3: Explore—Students apply research to design and test a model, process, or system to solve the problem presented in the challenge.

Step #4: Communicate—Students share results.

Step #5: Evaluate—Students are given an opportunity to reflect on what they have learned.

Managing the Lab

- Set a deadline for project submission and presentations.
- Group students into collaborative teams and assign roles.
- Review prerequisite skills students need for doing the lab, such as measuring, weighing, constructing, recording data, graphing, and so on.
- Review science safety rules.
- Review lab cleanup procedures.
- Have the needed materials available, organized, and set up for easy access.
- Monitor teams and provide productive feedback.
- Leave enough time at the end of class for cleanup and debriefing.
- Designate area for project storage.

Evaluation

Student Reflection: Students think about their team's choices for the design of the prototype. Students individually complete the "Reflection" handout.

Student Self-Evaluation: Students think about their behavior and performance as a team member. Students individually complete the "Self-Evaluation Rubric."

Lab Evaluation: The teacher completes the "Lab Challenge Rubric" for each team member.

Conference: Teacher/student conferences are held to discuss the completed evaluations.

Forces and Motion

3-D Pop Ups: Student Challenge

STEM Lab Challenge: Design a pop-up card that incorporates origami.

You Should Know

The design and creation of cards and books in art form is sometimes called "paper engineering."

Vocabulary Review

- force
- lever
- simple machines

Materials You May Need

- an assortment of colored copy paper
- an assortment of colored construction paper
- tape
- glue
- scissors
- ruler
- markers or colored pencils
- other design materials: to be determined by student research

Challenge Requirements

1. <u>Research</u>: Write a one- to two-page paper summarizing your research on pop-up card mechanisms and origami. Cite your sources. Your paper may include two pictures.
2. <u>Model</u>: Label a drawing of your card design and explain your strategy.
3. <u>Results</u>: Record, analyze, and interpret test results.
4. <u>Conclusion</u>: Summarize the lab and what actually happened. It should include the purpose, a brief description of the test procedure, and explanation of results.
5. <u>Reflection</u>: Think about your team's choices for the card design. Then complete the "Reflection" handout.
6. <u>Evaluation</u>: Think about your behavior and performance as a team member. Then complete the "Self-Evaluation Rubric."

Steps to Follow

Work with a team to complete the steps listed below. A team will have 3 or 4 members.

Step 1: Research pop-up card mechanisms and origami.
Step 2: Brainstorm ideas about how to design your card to meet the requirements of the lab. Think about the materials to use in your design.
Step 3: Draw a diagram of your card design.
Step 4: Construct the card.
Step 5: Test the card.
Step 6: Evaluate the performance of your card.
Step 7: Identify how to improve the design of your card.
Step 8: Make the needed changes.
Step 9: Retest and reevaluate the improved card.
Step 10: Share the results.

Aerodynamics of Paper Airplanes: Teacher Information

STEM Lab Overview

Students are challenged to design a paper airplane that will stay airborne for 10 seconds.

Concepts

- Aerodynamics
- Bernoulli's Principle

Standards for Grades 6–8

NGSS	NCTM	ITEA	CCSS
-Force and Interactions	-Problem Solving -Communication -Connections -Representation	-Nature of Technology -Technology and Society -Technological World	-English Language Arts Standards: Science & Technical Subjects

Teaching Strategies

Step #1: Engage—Review concepts. Introduce the STEM lab. Discuss the challenge presented in the lab, providing students with an opportunity to connect previous knowledge to the problem they are to solve.

Step #2: Investigate—Students conduct research to gain an understanding of the major science concepts related to the topic, review possible solutions to the lab challenge, and formulate new ideas for solving the problem.

Step #3: Explore—Students apply research to design and test a model, process, or system to solve the problem presented in the challenge.

Step #4: Communicate—Students share results.

Step #5: Evaluate—Students are given an opportunity to reflect on what they have learned.

Managing the Lab

- Set a deadline for project submission and presentations.
- Group students into collaborative teams and assign roles.
- Review prerequisite skills students need for doing the lab, such as measuring, weighing, constructing, recording data, graphing, and so on.
- Review science safety rules.
- Review lab cleanup procedures.
- Have the needed materials available, organized, and set up for easy access.
- Monitor teams and provide productive feedback.
- Leave enough time at the end of class for cleanup and debriefing.
- Designate area for project storage.

Evaluation

Student Reflection: Students think about their team's choices for the design of the prototype. Students individually complete the "Reflection" handout.

Student Self-Evaluation: Students think about their behavior and performance as a team member. Students individually complete the "Self-Evaluation Rubric."

Lab Evaluation: The teacher completes the "Lab Challenge Rubric" for each team member.

Conference: Teacher/student conferences are held to discuss the completed evaluations.

41

Aerodynamics of Paper Airplanes: Student Challenge

STEM Lab Challenge: Design a paper airplane that will stay airborne for 10 seconds.

You Should Know
Daniel Bernoulli (1700–1782) was a Dutch-Swiss mathematician. His most important work describes the relationship between fluid flow, pressure, and velocity.

Vocabulary Review
- aerodynamics
- Bernoulli's Principle
- drag
- lift
- thrust

Materials You May Need
- sheets of copy paper
- stopwatch
- scissors
- tape
- paper clips
- glue
- design materials: to be determined by student research

Challenge Requirements
1. <u>Research</u>: Write a one- to two-page paper summarizing your research on aerodynamics and Bernoulli's Principle. Cite your sources. Your paper may include two pictures.
2. <u>Model</u>: Label a drawing of your paper airplane design and explain your strategy.
3. <u>Results</u>: Record, analyze, and interpret test results.
4. <u>Conclusion</u>: Summarize the lab and what actually happened. It should include the purpose, a brief description of the test procedure, and explanation of results.
5. <u>Reflection</u>: Think about your team's choices for the design of the paper airplane. Then complete the "Reflection" handout.
6. <u>Evaluation</u>: Think about your behavior and performance as a team member. Then complete the "Self-Evaluation Rubric."

Steps to Follow
Work with a team to complete the steps listed below. A team will have 3 or 4 members.

Step 1: Research aerodynamics and Bernoulli's Principle.
Step 2: Brainstorm ideas about how to design a paper airplane to meet the requirements of the lab. Think about the shape of your plane. Some shapes are more aerodynamic than others.
Step 3: Draw a diagram of your design.
Step 4: Construct the paper airplane.
Step 5: Test the design.
Step 6: Evaluate the performance of your airplane.
Step 7: Identify how to improve your design.
Step 8: Make the needed changes.
Step 9: Retest and reevaluate the design.
Step 10: Share the results.

Newton's Blast-Off!: Teacher Information

STEM Lab Overview

Students are challenged to design a rocket, which is powered by pressure produced from an effervescing antacid tablet, that will travel to the height of 5 meters.

Concepts

• Newton's Laws of Motion

Standards for Grades 6–8

NGSS	NCTM	ITEA	CCSS
-Force and Interactions	-Problem Solving -Communication -Connections -Representation	-Nature of Technology -Technology and Society -Technological World	-English Language Arts Standards: Science & Technical Subjects

Teaching Strategies

Step #1: Engage—Review concepts. Introduce the STEM lab. Discuss the challenge presented in the lab, providing students with an opportunity to connect previous knowledge to the problem they are to solve.

Step #2: Investigate—Students conduct research to gain an understanding of the major science concepts related to the topic, review possible solutions to the lab challenge, and formulate new ideas for solving the problem.

Step #3: Explore—Students apply research to design and test a model, process, or system to solve the problem presented in the challenge.

Step #4: Communicate—Students share results.

Step #5: Evaluate—Students are given an opportunity to reflect on what they have learned.

Managing the Lab

• Set a deadline for project submission and presentations.
• Group students into collaborative teams and assign roles.
• Review prerequisite skills students need for doing the lab, such as measuring, weighing, constructing, recording data, graphing, and so on.
• Review science safety rules.
• Review lab cleanup procedures.
• Have the needed materials available, organized, and set up for easy access.
• Monitor teams and provide productive feedback.
• Leave enough time at the end of class for cleanup and debriefing.
• Designate area for project storage.

Evaluation

Student Reflection: Students think about their team's choices for the design of the prototype. Students individually complete the "Reflection" handout.

Student Self-Evaluation: Students think about their behavior and performance as a team member. Students individually complete the "Self-Evaluation Rubric."

Lab Evaluation: The teacher completes the "Lab Challenge Rubric" for each team member.

Conference: Teacher/student conferences are held to discuss the completed evaluations.

Newton's Blast-Off!: Student Challenge

STEM Lab Challenge: Design a rocket powered by pressure, which is produced from an effervescing antacid tablet, that will travel to the height of 5 meters.

You Should Know

NASA uses rockets to launch satellites and to send probes to outer space. The new rockets that are being developed today may someday send humans to Mars.

Vocabulary Review

- acceleration
- force
- friction
- gravity
- inertia
- Newton's Laws of Motion
- mass
- speed

Materials You May Need

- safety goggles
- card stock
- effervescing antacid tablet
- film canister (35 mm) with lid that snaps inside
- scissors
- tape
- water

Challenge Requirements

1. <u>Research</u>: Write a one- to two-page paper summarizing your research on Newton's Laws of Motion and rocket design. Cite your sources. Your paper may include two pictures.
2. <u>Model</u>: Label a drawing of your rocket design and explain your strategy.
3. <u>Results</u>: Record, analyze, and interpret test results.
4. <u>Conclusion</u>: Summarize the lab and what actually happened. It should include the purpose, a brief description of the test procedure, and explanation of results.
5. <u>Reflection</u>: Think about your team's choices for the rocket design. Then complete the "Reflection" handout.
6. <u>Evaluation</u>: Think about your behavior and performance as a team member. Then complete the "Self-Evaluation Rubric."

Steps to Follow

Work with a team to complete the steps listed below. A team will have 3 or 4 members.

Step 1: Research Newton's Laws of Motion and rocket design.
Step 2: Brainstorm ideas about how to meet the requirements of the lab. Think about how size and weight of the rocket will affect performance. Consider how the amount of tablet used will influence the height your rocket will travel.
Step 3: Draw a diagram of your design.
Step 4: Construct the rocket.
Step 5: Test the rocket.
Step 6: Evaluate the performance of your rocket design.
Step 7: Identify how to improve the design of your rocket.
Step 8: Make the needed changes.
Step 9: Retest and reevaluate the improved design.
Step 10: Share the results.

Forces and Motion

Scream Machine: Teacher Information

STEM Lab Overview

Students are challenged to design a roller coaster with 1 loop and 1 hill the height of 1 meter. A marble will complete the entire track without stopping or leaving the track within 5 seconds.

Concepts

- Forms of energy
- Law of Conservation of Energy

Standards for Grades 6–8

NGSS	NCTM	ITEA	CCSS
-Energy	-Problem Solving -Communication -Connections -Representation	-Nature of Technology -Technology and Society -Technological World	-English Language Arts Standards: Science & Technical Subjects

Teaching Strategies

Step #1: Engage—Review concepts. Introduce the STEM lab. Discuss the challenge presented in the lab, providing students with an opportunity to connect previous knowledge to the problem they are to solve.

Step #2: Investigate—Students conduct research to gain an understanding of the major science concepts related to the topic, review possible solutions to the lab challenge, and formulate new ideas for solving the problem.

Step #3: Explore—Students apply research to design and test a model, process, or system to solve the problem presented in the challenge.

Step #4: Communicate—Students share results.

Step #5: Evaluate—Students are given an opportunity to reflect on what they have learned.

Managing the Lab

- Set a deadline for project submission and presentations.
- Group students into collaborative teams and assign roles.
- Review prerequisite skills students need for doing the lab, such as measuring, weighing, constructing, recording data, graphing, and so on.
- Review science safety rules.
- Review lab cleanup procedures.
- Have the needed materials available, organized, and set up for easy access.
- Monitor teams and provide productive feedback.
- Leave enough time at the end of class for cleanup and debriefing.
- Designate area for project storage.

Evaluation

Student Reflection: Students think about their team's choices for the design of the prototype. Students individually complete the "Reflection" handout.

Student Self-Evaluation: Students think about their behavior and performance as a team member. Students individually complete the "Self-Evaluation Rubric."

Lab Evaluation: The teacher completes the "Lab Challenge Rubric" for each team member.

Conference: Teacher/student conferences are held to discuss the completed evaluations.

Scream Machine: Student Challenge

STEM Lab Challenge: Design a roller coaster with 1 loop and 1 hill the height of 1 meter. A marble will complete the entire track without stopping or leaving the track within 5 seconds.

You Should Know
The roller coaster is often referred to as the "scream machine." It was a ride developed for amusement parks. It does not have an engine but instead is powered by the conversion of potential energy to kinetic energy.

Vocabulary Review
- energy
- friction
- gravity
- kinetic energy
- Law of Conservation of Energy
- potential energy

Materials You May Need
- marbles
- cardboard
- an assortment of tubing
- string
- tape
- glue
- stopwatch
- blocks of wood or bricks
- other design materials: to be determined by student research

Challenge Requirements
1. <u>Research</u>: Write a one- to two-page paper summarizing your research on roller coasters and potential and kinetic energy. Cite your sources. Your paper may include two pictures.
2. <u>Model</u>: Label a drawing of your roller coaster design and explain your strategy.
3. <u>Results</u>: Record, analyze, and interpret test results.
4. <u>Conclusion</u>: Summarize the lab and what actually happened. It should include the purpose, a brief description of the test procedure, and explanation of results.
5. <u>Reflection</u>: Think about your team's choices for the roller coaster. Then complete the "Reflection" handout.
6. <u>Evaluation</u>: Think about your behavior and performance as a team member. Then complete the "Self-Evaluation Rubric."

Steps to Follow
Work with a team to complete the steps listed below. A team will have 3 or 4 members.

Step 1: Research roller coasters and potential and kinetic energy.
Step 2: Brainstorm ideas about how to design a roller coaster to meet the requirements of the lab. Think about the materials to use in your design.
Step 3: Draw a diagram of your design.
Step 4: Construct the roller coaster.
Step 5: Test the design.
Step 6: Evaluate the performance of your roller coaster.
Step 7: Identify how to improve your design.
Step 8: Make the needed changes.
Step 9: Retest and reevaluate your design.
Step 10: Share the results.

Is it Magic?: Teacher Information

STEM Lab Overview
Students are challenged to design a thaumatrope toy that will create an optical illusion.

Concepts
• Light   • Persistence of vision

Standards for Grades 6–8

NGSS	NCTM	ITEA	CCSS
-Waves and Electromagnetic Radiation	-Problem Solving -Communication -Connections -Representation	-Nature of Technology -Technology and Society -Technological World	-English Language Arts Standards: Science & Technical Subjects

Teaching Strategies

Step #1: Engage—Review concepts. Introduce the STEM lab. Discuss the challenge presented in the lab, providing students with an opportunity to connect previous knowledge to the problem they are to solve.

Step #2: Investigate—Students conduct research to gain an understanding of the major science concepts related to the topic, review possible solutions to the lab challenge, and formulate new ideas for solving the problem.

Step #3: Explore—Students apply research to design and test a model, process, or system to solve the problem presented in the challenge.

Step #4: Communicate—Students share results.

Step #5: Evaluate—Students are given an opportunity to reflect on what they have learned.

Managing the Lab

• Set a deadline for project submission and presentations.
• Group students into collaborative teams and assign roles.
• Review prerequisite skills students need for doing the lab, such as measuring, weighing, constructing, recording data, graphing, and so on.
• Review science safety rules.
• Review lab cleanup procedures.
• Have the needed materials available, organized, and set up for easy access.
• Monitor teams and provide productive feedback.
• Leave enough time at the end of class for cleanup and debriefing.
• Designate area for project storage.

Evaluation

Student Reflection: Students think about their team's choices for the design of the prototype. Students individually complete the "Reflection" handout.

Student Self-Evaluation: Students think about their behavior and performance as a team member. Students individually complete the "Self-Evaluation Rubric."

Lab Evaluation: The teacher completes the "Lab Challenge Rubric" for each team member.

Conference: Teacher/student conferences are held to discuss the completed evaluations.

Energy

Is it Magic?: Student Challenge

STEM Lab Challenge: Design a thaumatrope toy that will create an optical illusion.

You Should Know
The thaumatrope was invented in 1826 by the English physician J.A. Paris. It was an optical illusion instrument he used to explore persistence of vision. The device consisted of a piece of cardboard with a picture or image on each side and two pieces of string attached to the cardboard. When the string was rapidly twisted back and forth, the pictures on either side combined into one.

Vocabulary Review
- light
- optical illusion
- persistence of vision

Materials You May Need
- crayons or markers
- white cardboard
- cottage cheese or sour cream lid
- string
- pointed scissors
- tape
- glue
- bamboo skewers

Challenge Requirements
1. <u>Research</u>: Write a one- to two-page paper summarizing your research on light, persistence of vision, and optical illusions. Cite your sources. Your paper may include two pictures.
2. <u>Model</u>: Label a drawing of your toy and explain your strategy.
3. <u>Results</u>: Record, analyze, and interpret test results.
4. <u>Conclusion</u>: Summarize the lab and what actually happened. It should include the purpose, a brief description of the test procedure, and explanation of results.
5. <u>Reflection</u>: Think about your team's choices for the toy design. Then complete the "Reflection" handout.
6. <u>Evaluation</u>: Think about your behavior and performance as a team member. Then complete the "Self-Evaluation Rubric."

Steps to Follow
Work with a team to complete the steps listed below. A team will have 3 or 4 members.

Step 1: Research light, persistence of vision, and optical illusions.

Step 2: Brainstorm ideas about how to design a toy to meet the requirements of the lab. Think about how you will test your toy.

Step 3: Draw a diagram of your toy.

Step 4: Construct the toy.

Step 5: Test the toy.

Step 6: Evaluate the performance of your toy.

Step 7: Identify how to improve the design of your toy.

Step 8: Make the needed changes.

Step 9: Retest and reevaluate the improved toy.

Step 10: Share the results.

Boomerang Can Toy: Teacher Information

STEM Lab Overview

Students are challenged to design a coffee-can toy to demonstrate how energy, work, and power are related.

Concepts

- Energy transfer
- Forms of energy
- Law of Conservation of Energy

Standards for Grades 6–8			
NGSS	**NCTM**	**ITEA**	**CCSS**
-Energy	-Problem Solving -Communication -Connections -Representation	-Nature of Technology -Technology and Society -Technological World	-English Language Arts Standards: Science & Technical Subjects

Teaching Strategies

Step #1: Engage—Review concepts. Introduce the STEM lab. Discuss the challenge presented in the lab, providing students with an opportunity to connect previous knowledge to the problem they are to solve.

Step #2: Investigate—Students conduct research to gain an understanding of the major science concepts related to the topic, review possible solutions to the lab challenge, and formulate new ideas for solving the problem.

Step #3: Explore Students apply research to design and test a model, process, or system to solve the problem presented in the challenge.

Step #4: Communicate—Students share results.

Step #5: Evaluate—Students are given an opportunity to reflect on what they have learned.

Managing the Lab

- Set a deadline for project submission and presentations.
- Group students into collaborative teams and assign roles.
- Review prerequisite skills students need for doing the lab, such as measuring, weighing, constructing, recording data, graphing, and so on.
- Review science safety rules.
- Review lab cleanup procedures.
- Have the needed materials available, organized, and set up for easy access.
- Monitor teams and provide productive feedback.
- Leave enough time at the end of class for cleanup and debriefing.
- Designate area for project storage.

Evaluation

Student Reflection: Students think about their team's choices for the design of the prototype. Students individually complete the "Reflection" handout.

Student Self-Evaluation: Students think about their behavior and performance as a team member. Students individually complete the "Self-Evaluation Rubric."

Lab Evaluation: The teacher completes the "Lab Challenge Rubric" for each team member.

Conference: Teacher/student conferences are held to discuss the completed evaluations.

Boomerang Can Toy: Student Challenge

STEM Lab Challenge: Design a coffee-can toy that when rolled away from you will stop on its own and then roll back to you.

You Should Know
Wind-up toys were first mass-produced in Europe in the late 1880s. The next 60 to 70 years, manufacturers made more intricately designed wind-ups. In the 1960s, alkaline batteries powered small motors, thus, replacing the wind-up mechanism. Wind-up toys soon lost popularity.

Vocabulary Review
- energy
- elastic potential energy
- Law of Conservation of Energy
- mechanical kinetic energy
- mechanical potential energy

Materials You May Need
- coffee can or oatmeal container with lid
- metal nut
- two paper clips
- rubber band
- pencil or pen

Challenge Requirements
1. <u>Research</u>: Write a one- to two-page paper summarizing your research on potential and kinetic energy. Cite your sources. Your paper may include two pictures.
2. <u>Model</u>: Label a drawing of your toy design and explain your strategy.
3. <u>Results</u>: Record, analyze, and interpret test results.
4. <u>Conclusion</u>: Summarize the lab and what actually happened. It should include the purpose, a brief description of the test procedure, and explanation of results.
5. <u>Reflection</u>: Think about your team's choices for the toy design. Then complete the "Reflection" handout.
6. <u>Evaluation</u>: Think about your behavior and performance as a team member. Then complete the "Self-Evaluation Rubric."

Steps to Follow
Work with a team to complete the steps listed below. A team will have 3 or 4 members.

Step 1: Research mechanical potential and mechanical kinetic energy.
Step 2: Brainstorm ideas about how to meet the requirements of the lab. Think about how to make your toy roll back to you.
Step 3: Draw a diagram of your toy design.
Step 4: Create the toy.
Step 5: Test the toy.
Step 6: Evaluate the performance of your toy.
Step 7: Identify how to improve the design of your toy.
Step 8: Make the needed changes.
Step 9: Retest and reevaluate the improved toy.
Step 10: Share the results.

Electric Maze: Teacher Information

STEM Lab Overview
Students are challenged to design an electrical-circuit maze that will signal with a light when the circuit has been closed.

Concepts
• Electricity   • Electric circuits   • Current electricity

Standards for Grades 6–8

NGSS	NCTM	ITEA	CCSS
-Energy	-Problem Solving -Communication -Connections -Representation	-Nature of Technology -Technology and Society -Technological World	-English Language Arts Standards: Science & Technical Subjects

Teaching Strategies

Step #1: Engage—Review concepts. Introduce the STEM lab. Discuss the challenge presented in the lab, providing students with an opportunity to connect previous knowledge to the problem they are to solve.

Step #2: Investigate—Students conduct research to gain an understanding of the major science concepts related to the topic, review possible solutions to the lab challenge, and formulate new ideas for solving the problem.

Step #3: Explore—Students apply research to design and test a model, process, or system to solve the problem presented in the challenge.

Step #4: Communicate—Students share results.

Step #5: Evaluate—Students are given an opportunity to reflect on what they have learned.

Managing the Lab

• Set a deadline for project submission and presentations.
• Group students into collaborative teams and assign roles.
• Review prerequisite skills students need for doing the lab, such as measuring, weighing, constructing, recording data, graphing, and so on.
• Review science safety rules.
• Review lab cleanup procedures.
• Have the needed materials available, organized, and set up for easy access.
• Monitor teams and provide productive feedback.
• Leave enough time at the end of class for cleanup and debriefing.
• Designate area for project storage.

Evaluation

Student Reflection: Students think about their team's choices for the design of the prototype. Students individually complete the "Reflection" handout.

Student Self-Evaluation: Students think about their behavior and performance as a team member. Students individually complete the "Self-Evaluation Rubric."

Lab Evaluation: The teacher completes the "Lab Challenge Rubric" for each team member.

Conference: Teacher/student conferences are held to discuss the completed evaluations.

Electric Maze: Student Challenge

STEM Lab Challenge: Design an electrical-circuit maze that will signal with a light when the circuit has been closed.

You Should Know
An electric circuit is a pathway for electricity to flow. Electricity can only flow when the circuit is complete with no breaks or gaps.

Vocabulary Review
- closed circuit
- electrical current
- electricity
- open circuit
- series circuit
- switches

Materials You May Need
- block of wood
- wire
- wire cutters
- hammer
- batteries
- bulb in a bulb holder
- tape
- paper clip
- other design materials: to be determined by student research

Challenge Requirements
1. <u>Research</u>: Write a one- to two-page paper summarizing your research on electricity and electrical circuits. Cite your sources. Your paper may include two pictures.
2. <u>Model</u>: Label a drawing of your electrical maze design and explain your strategy.
3. <u>Results</u>: Record, analyze, and interpret test results.
4. <u>Conclusion</u>: Summarize the lab and what actually happened. It should include the purpose, a brief description of the test procedure, and explanation of results.
5. <u>Reflection</u>: Think about your team's choices for the electrical maze design. Then complete the "Reflection" handout.
6. <u>Evaluation</u>: Think about your behavior and performance as a team member. Then complete the "Self-Evaluation Rubric."

Steps to Follow
Work with a team to complete the steps listed below. A team will have 3 or 4 members.

Step 1: Research electricity and electrical circuits.

Step 2: Brainstorm ideas about how to design your electrical maze to meet the requirements of the lab. Think about the shape of your maze.

Step 3: Draw a diagram of your design.

Step 4: Construct the electrical maze.

Step 5: Test the design.

Step 6: Evaluate the performance of your electrical maze.

Step 7: Identify how to improve your design.

Step 8: Make the needed changes.

Step 9: Retest and reevaluate the design.

Step 10: Share the results.

Magnetic Game: Teacher Information

STEM Lab Overview

Students are challenged to design a race car board game where the players move the game pieces around the track using magnetic force.

Concepts

• Magnets   • Magnetism

Standards for Grades 6–8

NGSS	NCTM	ITEA	CCSS
-Energy	-Problem Solving -Communication -Connections -Representation	-Nature of Technology -Technology and Society -Technological World	-English Language Arts Standards: Science & Technical Subjects

Teaching Strategies

Step #1:   Engage—Review concepts. Introduce the STEM lab. Discuss the challenge presented in the lab, providing students with an opportunity to connect previous knowledge to the problem they are to solve.

Step #2:   Investigate—Students conduct research to gain an understanding of the major science concepts related to the topic, review possible solutions to the lab challenge, and formulate new ideas for solving the problem.

Step #3:   Explore—Students apply research to design and test a model, process, or system to solve the problem presented in the challenge.

Step #4:   Communicate—Students share results.

Step #5:   Evaluate—Students are given an opportunity to reflect on what they have learned.

Managing the Lab

• Set a deadline for project submission and presentations.
• Group students into collaborative teams and assign roles.
• Review prerequisite skills students need for doing the lab, such as measuring, weighing, constructing, recording data, graphing, and so on.
• Review science safety rules.
• Review lab cleanup procedures.
• Have the needed materials available, organized, and set up for easy access.
• Monitor teams and provide productive feedback.
• Leave enough time at the end of class for cleanup and debriefing.
• Designate area for project storage.

Evaluation

Student Reflection: Students think about their team's choices for the design of the prototype. Students individually complete the "Reflection" handout.

Student Self-Evaluation: Students think about their behavior and performance as a team member. Students individually complete the "Self-Evaluation Rubric."

Lab Evaluation: The teacher completes the "Lab Challenge Rubric" for each team member.

Conference: Teacher/student conferences are held to discuss the completed evaluations.

Magnetic Game: Student Challenge

STEM Lab Challenge: Design a race car board game where the players move the game pieces around the track using magnetic force.

You Should Know

The first magnets used by people were called lodestones. Lodestone, or iron ore, is also called magnetite and is found naturally on the earth's surface.

Vocabulary Review

- attract
- magnet
- magnetic field
- magnetic force
- repel

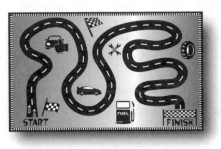

Materials You May Need

- cardboard
- tape
- markers
- scissors
- wooden dowel rods
- an assortment of magnets
- other design materials: to be determined by student research

Challenge Requirements

1. <u>Research</u>: Write a one- to two-page paper summarizing your research on magnets and magnetism. Cite your sources. Your paper may include two pictures.
2. <u>Model</u>: Label a drawing of your design and explain your strategy.
3. <u>Results</u>: Record, analyze, and interpret test results.
4. <u>Conclusion</u>: Summarize the lab and what actually happened. It should include the purpose, a brief description of the test procedure, and explanation of results.
5. <u>Reflection</u>: Think about your team's choices for the game design. Then complete the "Reflection" handout.
6. <u>Evaluation</u>: Think about your behavior and performance as a team member. Then complete the "Self-Evaluation Rubric."

Steps to Follow

Work with a team to complete the steps listed below. A team will have 3 or 4 members.

Step 1: Research magnets and magnetism.
Step 2: Brainstorm ideas about how to design a magnetic game to meet the requirements of the lab. Think about how you will make the game pieces move by magnetic force on your gameboard.
Step 3: Draw a diagram of your design.
Step 4: Construct the game.
Step 5: Test the design.
Step 6: Evaluate the performance of your game.
Step 7: Identify how to improve your design.
Step 8: Make the needed changes.
Step 9: Retest and reevaluate the design.
Step 10: Share the results.

Dance! Dance! Dance!: Teacher Information

STEM Lab Overview

Students are challenged to design a dance mat that lights up or sounds a buzzer when stepped on.

Concepts

- Electricity
- Electrical circuits
- Current electricity

Standards for Grades 6–8

NGSS	NCTM	ITEA	CCSS
-Energy -Waves and Electromagnetic Radiation	-Problem Solving -Communication -Connections -Representation	-Nature of Technology -Technology and Society -Technological World	-English Language Arts Standards: Science & Technical Subjects

Teaching Strategies

Step #1: Engage—Review concepts. Introduce the STEM lab. Discuss the challenge presented in the lab, providing students with an opportunity to connect previous knowledge to the problem they are to solve.

Step #2: Investigate—Students conduct research to gain an understanding of the major science concepts related to the topic, review possible solutions to the lab challenge, and formulate new ideas for solving the problem.

Step #3: Explore—Students apply research to design and test a model, process, or system to solve the problem presented in the challenge.

Step #4: Communicate—Students share results.

Step #5: Evaluate—Students are given an opportunity to reflect on what they have learned.

Managing the Lab

- Set a deadline for project submission and presentations.
- Group students into collaborative teams and assign roles.
- Review prerequisite skills students need for doing the lab, such as measuring, weighing, constructing, recording data, graphing, and so on.
- Review science safety rules.
- Review lab cleanup procedures.
- Have the needed materials available, organized, and set up for easy access.
- Monitor teams and provide productive feedback.
- Leave enough time at the end of class for cleanup and debriefing.
- Designate area for project storage.

Evaluation

Student Reflection: Students think about their team's choices for the design of the prototype. Students individually complete the "Reflection" handout.

Student Self-Evaluation: Students think about their behavior and performance as a team member. Students individually complete the "Self-Evaluation Rubric."

Lab Evaluation: The teacher completes the "Lab Challenge Rubric" for each team member.

Conference: Teacher/student conferences are held to discuss the completed evaluations.

Dance! Dance! Dance!: Student Challenge

STEM Lab Challenge: Design a dance mat that lights up or sounds a buzzer when stepped on.

You Should Know

Electricity flows in an electrical circuit called a pathway. This electricity can only flow when the circuit is complete with no breaks or gaps in the pathways.

Vocabulary Review

- closed circuit
- conductors
- electrical circuit
- electricity
- insulator
- open circuit
- resistance
- resistor
- series circuit
- switches

Materials You May Need

- batteries
- wire cutters
- tape
- wire
- corrugated cardboard
- bulbs with holders
- buzzers
- scissors
- other design materials: to be determined by student research

Challenge Requirements

1. <u>Research</u>: Write a one- to two-page paper summarizing your research on electronic dance mats and electrical circuits. Cite your sources. Your paper may include two pictures.
2. <u>Model</u>: Label a drawing of your dance mat design and explain your strategy.
3. <u>Results</u>: Record, analyze, and interpret test results.
4. <u>Conclusion</u>: Summarize the lab and what actually happened. It should include the purpose, a brief description of the test procedure, and explanation of results.
5. <u>Reflection</u>: Think about your team's choices for the dance mat design. Then complete the "Reflection" handout.
6. <u>Evaluation</u>: Think about your behavior and performance as a team member. Then complete the "Self-Evaluation Rubric."

Steps to Follow

Work with a team to complete the steps listed below. A team will have 3 or 4 members.

Step 1: Research electronic dance mats and electrical circuits.
Step 2: Brainstorm ideas about how to design your dance mat to meet the requirements of the lab. Think about the materials to use in your design.
Step 3: Draw a diagram of your mat design.
Step 4: Construct the mat.
Step 5: Test the mat.
Step 6: Evaluate the performance of your mat.
Step 7: Identify how to improve the design of your mat.
Step 8: Make the needed changes.
Step 9: Retest and reevaluate the improved mat.
Step 10: Share the results.

Play That Tune: Teacher Information

STEM Lab Overview
Students are challenged to design a musical instrument able to play a simple tune.

Concepts
• Energy   • Sound

Standards for Grades 6–8			
NGSS	**NCTM**	**ITEA**	**CCSS**

-Energy
-Waves and
  Electromagnetic
  Radiation
	-Problem Solving
	-Communication
	-Connections
	-Representation
		-Nature of Technology
		-Technology and
		  Society
		-Technological World
			-English Language Arts
			  Standards:
			  Science & Technical
			  Subjects

Teaching Strategies

Step #1:   Engage—Review concepts. Introduce the STEM lab. Discuss the challenge presented in the lab, providing students with an opportunity to connect previous knowledge to the problem they are to solve.

Step #2:   Investigate—Students conduct research to gain an understanding of the major science concepts related to the topic, review possible solutions to the lab challenge, and formulate new ideas for solving the problem.

Step #3:   Explore—Students apply research to design and test a model, process, or system to solve the problem presented in the challenge.

Step #4:   Communicate—Students share results.

Step #5:   Evaluate—Students are given an opportunity to reflect on what they have learned.

Managing the Lab

- Set a deadline for project submission and presentations.
- Group students into collaborative teams and assign roles.
- Review prerequisite skills students need for doing the lab, such as measuring, weighing, constructing, recording data, graphing, and so on.
- Review science safety rules.
- Review lab cleanup procedures.
- Have the needed materials available, organized, and set up for easy access.
- Monitor teams and provide productive feedback.
- Leave enough time at the end of class for cleanup and debriefing.
- Designate area for project storage.

Evaluation

Student Reflection: Students think about their team's choices for the design of the prototype. Students individually complete the "Reflection" handout.

Student Self-Evaluation: Students think about their behavior and performance as a team member. Students individually complete the "Self-Evaluation Rubric."

Lab Evaluation: The teacher completes the "Lab Challenge Rubric" for each team member.

Conference: Teacher/student conferences are held to discuss the completed evaluations.

Play That Tune: Student Challenge

STEM Lab Challenge: Design a musical instrument able to play a simple tune.

You Should Know
Sound is a form of energy. Two major ways in which sound can vary are pitch and volume.

Vocabulary Review
- amplitude
- compression wave
- energy transfer
- frequency
- longitudinal wave
- pitch
- sound
- vibration
- volume

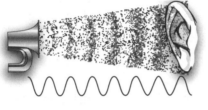

Materials You May Need
- design materials: to be determined by student research

Challenge Requirements
1. <u>Research</u>: Write a one- to two-page paper summarizing your research on sound and musical instruments. Cite your sources. Your paper may include two pictures.
2. <u>Model</u>: Label a drawing of your musical instrument design and explain your strategy.
3. <u>Results</u>: Record, analyze, and interpret test results.
4. <u>Conclusion</u>: Summarize the lab and what actually happened. It should include the purpose, a brief description of the test procedure, and explanation of results.
5. <u>Reflection</u>: Think about your team's choices for the design of the musical instrument. Then complete the "Reflection" handout.
6. <u>Evaluation</u>: Think about your behavior and performance as a team member. Then complete the "Self-Evaluation Rubric."

Steps to Follow
Work with a team to complete the steps listed below. A team will have 3 or 4 members.

Step 1: Research sound and musical instruments.
Step 2: Brainstorm ideas about how to design a musical instrument to meet the requirements of the lab. Think about the materials to use in your design.
Step 3: Draw a diagram of your design.
Step 4: Construct the musical instrument.
Step 5: Test the design.
Step 6: Evaluate the performance of your musical instrument.
Step 7: Identify how to improve your design.
Step 8: Make the needed changes.
Step 9: Retest and reevaluate the design.
Step 10: Share the results.

Light Controller: Teacher Information

STEM Lab Overview

Students are challenged to design an electrical circuit that dims a light bulb.

Concepts

- Electricity
- Electrical circuits
- Current electricity
- Resistor

Standards for Grades 6–8

NGSS	NCTM	ITEA	CCSS

-Energy	-Problem Solving
	-Communication
	-Connections
	-Representation
		-Nature of Technology
		-Technology and
		  Society
		-Technological World
			-English Language Arts
			  Standards:
			  Science & Technical
			  Subjects

Teaching Strategies

Step #1: Engage—Review concepts. Introduce the STEM lab. Discuss the challenge presented in the lab, providing students with an opportunity to connect previous knowledge to the problem they are to solve.

Step #2: Investigate—Students conduct research to gain an understanding of the major science concepts related to the topic, review possible solutions to the lab challenge, and formulate new ideas for solving the problem.

Step #3: Explore—Students apply research to design and test a model, process, or system to solve the problem presented in the challenge.

Step #4: Communicate—Students share results.

Step #5: Evaluate—Students are given an opportunity to reflect on what they have learned.

Managing the Lab

- Set a deadline for project submission and presentations.
- Group students into collaborative teams and assign roles.
- Review prerequisite skills students need for doing the lab, such as measuring, weighing, constructing, recording data, graphing, and so on.
- Review science safety rules.
- Review lab cleanup procedures.
- Have the needed materials available, organized, and set up for easy access.
- Monitor teams and provide productive feedback.
- Leave enough time at the end of class for cleanup and debriefing.
- Designate area for project storage.

Evaluation

Student Reflection: Students think about their team's choices for the design of the prototype. Students individually complete the "Reflection" handout.

Student Self-Evaluation: Students think about their behavior and performance as a team member. Students individually complete the "Self-Evaluation Rubric."

Lab Evaluation: The teacher completes the "Lab Challenge Rubric" for each team member.

Conference: Teacher/student conferences are held to discuss the completed evaluations.

Energy

Light Controller: Student Challenge

STEM Lab Challenge: Design an electrical circuit that dims a light bulb.

You Should Know

Electricity flows in an electrical circuit called a pathway. This electricity can only flow when the circuit is complete with no breaks or gaps in the pathways. When a resistor is placed in the pathway, the moving electrical charge is affected.

Vocabulary Review

- closed circuit
- conductors
- electrical circuit
- electricity
- insulator
- open circuit
- resistance
- resistor
- semiconductor
- series circuit
- switches

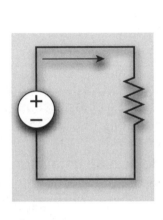

Materials You May Need

- battery
- wire cutters
- tape
- wire
- pencil lead
- bulb with holder
- alligator clips
- rubber tubing
- other design materials: to be determined by student research

Challenge Requirements

1. <u>Research</u>: Write a one- to two-page paper summarizing your research on electrical circuits and dimmer switches. Cite your sources. Your paper may include two pictures.
2. <u>Model</u>: Label a drawing of your circuit design and explain your strategy.
3. <u>Results</u>: Record, analyze, and interpret test results.
4. <u>Conclusion</u>: Summarize the lab and what actually happened. It should include the purpose, a brief description of the test procedure, and explanation of results.
5. <u>Reflection</u>: Think about your team's choices for the circuit design. Then complete the "Reflection" handout.
6. <u>Evaluation</u>: Think about your behavior and performance as a team member. Then complete the "Self-Evaluation Rubric."

Steps to Follow

Work with a team to complete the steps listed below. A team will have 3 or 4 members.

Step 1: Research electrical circuits and dimmer switches.

Step 2: Brainstorm ideas about how to design your circuit to meet the requirements of the lab. Think about the materials to use in your design.

Step 3: Draw a diagram of your circuit design.

Step 4: Construct the circuit.

Step 5: Test the circuit.

Step 6: Evaluate the performance of your circuit.

Step 7: Identify how to improve the design of your circuit.

Step 8: Make the needed changes.

Step 9: Retest and reevaluate the improved circuit.

Step 10: Share the results.

Wilderness Kit: Teacher Information

STEM Lab Overview
Students are challenged to design a wilderness kit for hikers that includes the materials and directions for constructing a simple compass.

Concepts
• Magnets   • Magnetism

Standards for Grades 6–8

NGSS	NCTM	ITEA	CCSS
-Energy	-Problem Solving -Communication -Connections -Representation	-Nature of Technology -Technology and Society -Technological World	-English Language Arts Standards: Science & Technical Subjects

Teaching Strategies

Step #1: Engage—Review concepts. Introduce the STEM lab. Discuss the challenge presented in the lab, providing students with an opportunity to connect previous knowledge to the problem they are to solve.

Step #2: Investigate—Students conduct research to gain an understanding of the major science concepts related to the topic, review possible solutions to the lab challenge, and formulate new ideas for solving the problem.

Step #3: Explore—Students apply research to design and test a model, process, or system to solve the problem presented in the challenge.

Step #4: Communicate—Students share results.

Step #5: Evaluate—Students are given an opportunity to reflect on what they have learned.

Managing the Lab

- Set a deadline for project submission and presentations.
- Group students into collaborative teams and assign roles.
- Review prerequisite skills students need for doing the lab, such as measuring, weighing, constructing, recording data, graphing, and so on.
- Review science safety rules.
- Review lab cleanup procedures.
- Have the needed materials available, organized, and set up for easy access.
- Monitor teams and provide productive feedback.
- Leave enough time at the end of class for cleanup and debriefing.
- Designate area for project storage.

Evaluation

Student Reflection: Students think about their team's choices for the design of the prototype. Students individually complete the "Reflection" handout.

Student Self-Evaluation: Students think about their behavior and performance as a team member. Students individually complete the "Self-Evaluation Rubric."

Lab Evaluation: The teacher completes the "Lab Challenge Rubric" for each team member.

Conference: Teacher/student conferences are held to discuss the completed evaluations.

Wilderness Kit: Student Challenge

STEM Lab Challenge: Design a wilderness kit for hikers that includes the materials and directions for constructing a simple compass.

You Should Know

Chinese inventors were the first to discover a way to magnetize pieces of iron, nearly one thousand years ago. This led to a method to manufacture compasses. A compass can be a valuable tool for someone who has lost their direction.

Vocabulary Review

- attract
- magnet
- magnetic field
- magnetic force
- magnetism
- poles
- repel

Materials You May Need

- design materials: to be determined by student research

Challenge Requirements

1. <u>Research</u>: Write a one- to two-page paper summarizing your research on compasses and magnetism. Cite your sources. Your paper may include two pictures.
2. <u>Model</u>: Label a drawing of your compass design and explain your strategy.
3. <u>Results</u>: Record, analyze, and interpret test results.
4. <u>Conclusion</u>: Summarize the lab and what actually happened. It should include the purpose, a brief description of the test procedure, and explanation of results.
5. <u>Reflection</u>: Think about your team's choices for the wilderness kit design. Then complete the "Reflection" handout.
6. <u>Evaluation</u>: Think about your behavior and performance as a team member. Then complete the "Self-Evaluation Rubric."

Steps to Follow

Work with a team to complete the steps listed below. A team will have 3 or 4 members.

Step 1: Research compasses and magnetism.
Step 2: Brainstorm ideas about how to meet the requirements of the lab. Think about how to write clear and precise directions for constructing the compass.
Step 3: Draw a diagram of your compass design.
Step 4: Gather materials and create the kit. Construct the compass.
Step 5: Test the directions for constructing the compass and the reliability of the compass.
Step 6: Evaluate the performance of your wilderness kit.
Step 7: Identify how to improve the instructions and design for your compass.
Step 8: Make the needed changes.
Step 9: Retest and reevaluate the improved design.
Step 10: Share the results.